MASTERING UAE LABOUR LAW

A PRACTICAL GUIDE TO COMPLIANCE AND STRATEGY

RAGHWENDRA KUMAR VERMA
KAVITA GUJARATHI

INDIA • SINGAPORE • MALAYSIA

ISBN

Paperback 979-8-89544-579-2
Hardcase 979-8-89588-276-4

Contents

Chapter-I

Introduction

Employment Law, UAE

The United Arab Emirates published its new Federal Labour Law No. 33 of 2022. It is effective from 2nd February 2022. On 3rd February 2022, as per Article 72 of the New Federal law (The Decree Law), the Executive Regulations of Federal Decree Law No. 33 of 2021, regarding the regulation of labour relations, was published.

The UAE's new labour law is the most momentous change to the erstwhile UAE labour law, also known as Federal Law No. 8 of 1980.

The new labour law, first presented by the Emirati government in November 2021, intends to improve workplace flexibility, combat workplace discrimination and promote employee safety and efficiency.

The Minister of Human Resources and Emiratization (MOHRE), Dr Abdul Rahman Al Awar, stated that the new law intends to help the UAE's efforts to build a labour market that can adapt to the dynamic modern world. It seeks to meet the needs of employees and employers, protect employee rights, and improve the UAE's competitiveness in recruiting talent and expertise from around the world.

The Minister of Human Resources and Emiratization (MOHRE), His Excellency Dr Abdul Rahman Al Awar, Minister of Human Resources and Emiratization, said that the new law strengthens the position of the UAE labour market as one of the most prominent and important global labour markets that offers flexibility, efficiency, ease of work, and attraction of competencies, expertise, and skills, while protecting and guaranteeing the rights of both parties to the employment relationship in a balanced manner.

He added that the new law provides employers and employees with several options to determine the form and model of the contractual employment relationship in accordance with the wishes of both parties, especially given the existence of 12 types of work permits and 6 types of work models, under which contractual employment relationships are established.

As a result, the changes in the new Law require employers operating in the UAE to take the necessary steps to ensure compliance with the additional or amended provisions.

The issuance of the new Law aims to respond to the challenges and needs of the labour market, which has significantly evolved over the recent years. Additionally, the new Law reflects the UAE government's intention to implement a regulatory and statutory framework that is aligned with global standards.

Important changes introduced by this law are new work models, introduction of visa categories, limited employment contracts, non-compete, non-discrimination clause. Additional **leave for maternity, introduction of study leave, paternal leave, and workplace regulation, etc.**

Accordingly, through Article 73 of the decree law, Federal Law No. (8) of 1980 on the Regulation of Labour Relations shall be repealed, and any provision contrary to or in conflict with the provisions of the old Decree Law shall be repealed.

Decisions, regulations, and rules in force prior to the enactment of the provisions of this Decree Law shall continue to apply, to the extent that they do not conflict with the provisions hereof, until they are replaced in accordance with the provisions of this Decree Law.

Article 65 of the Decree Law, which deals with final provisions, emphasises the importance of this decree law. It is absolutely clear that the rights of workers prescribed under this law are minimum rights, and employers may provide more beneficial rights to workers than those prescribed under this law.

Article 65 says as follows:

1. Rights laid down in this Decree Law shall consist of the minimum worker's rights. The provisions of this Decree Law shall not prejudice any of the rights prescribed for workers under any other legislation, agreement, declaration, regulation or employment contract, giving rise to rights that are more beneficial than those laid down in the provisions of this Decree Law.

2. The Employer or worker may not misapply the provisions of this Decree Law and, its Executive Regulations and implementing resolutions, and neither of them may take any act which might put pressure on the other's freedom, or the freedom, of other workers or Employers; with the intent to achieve any interest or point of view contrary to the freedom of work or the jurisdiction of the competent authority to resolve dispute.

3. Any condition which is contrary to the provisions of this Decree Law, even if preceded by its entry into force, shall be null and void, unless it is more beneficial to the worker. Any release, conciliation or waiver of any rights of the worker hereunder shall be null and void to the extent that it conflicts with its provisions.

4. The Employer may establish and put in place organisational by-laws and programmes in the Establishment that would be more beneficial to the worker, than those prescribed in this Decree Law and its Executive Regulations. In the event of conflict between such

programmes and by-laws and the provisions of this Decree Law, conditions that are more beneficial to the worker shall apply.

5. The Employer may not review the terms and conditions of a valid employment contract concluded with the worker prior to the promulgation of this Decree Law, with the intent to apply the provisions hereof, unless such amendments are for the greater good and benefit of the worker. The employment contract may be updated after its expiration in accordance with the provisions of this Decree Law.

6. The Employer or worker may terminate the indefinite term contract entered into before the **entry into force of this Decree Law for a legal cause by giving the other (30) thirty days prior written notice if the period of service is less than (5) five years,** or **(60) sixty days prior written notice if the period of service exceeds (5) five years, or (90) ninety days prior written notice if the period of service exceeds (10) ten years.**

7. Payments due to the worker or the members of his family, under the provisions of this Decree Law shall have priority over all, Employer's funds and shall be paid promptly after the amount due to the public treasury and legal alimony awarded to the wife and children are paid.

Main Point:

1. Right of termination of an indefinite contract:

   - **(30) thirty days prior written notice if the period of service is less than (5) five years, or**

   - **(60) sixty days prior written notice if the period of service exceeds (5) five years, or**

   - **(90) ninety days prior written notice, if the period of service exceeds (10) ten years.**

2. **The rights of the worker prescribed under this law are minimum rights of the workers, and the employer may provide more beneficial rights to workers than those prescribed under this law.**

As Per Article 66 of this Decree Law, the Preferred Language shall be Arabic.

Arabic language shall be the language to be used in all records, files, statements, templates and any other documents set forth in this Decree Law and its Executive Regulations and implementing resolutions.

The Arabic shall also be used by the Employer in contracts concluded with workers, and instructions and circulars issued by him to workers, provided that **another language understood by a non-Arabic speaker is used beside Arabic. The Arabic text and foreign text shall be identical, and, in case of any conflict, the Arabic version shall prevail.**

As per Article 67 of this Decree law, Dates and periods of time stipulated herein shall be construed according to the **Gregorian calendar.** In the application of the provisions of this Decree Law, a calendar year, shall consist of **(365) three hundred sixty-five days,** and a month shall consist of **(30) thirty days.**

Through Article 68 of this Decree law, the employer has been given a window period during which they can align their work contracts and payment of gratuity as per this Decree law. Below are the provisions of Article 68.

1. The provisions of this Decree Law shall apply to indefinite term employment contracts concluded under the referenced Federal Law No. (8) of 1980.

2. Employers shall, within (1) one year from the date of entry into force of this Decree Law, adjust their respective positions and change indefinite term employment contracts to definite term employment contracts, in accordance with the conditions, controls, and procedures set forth herein. Such period may be extended by the Minister for other periods, as dictated by the public interest.

3. Subject to paragraph (2) above, the Employer may calculate the gratuity in accordance with the provisions of the indefinite term employment contract stated in the referenced Federal Law No. (8) of 1980.

Main Point

1. A one year window has been provided to change an indefinite contract to a definite contract.
2. Calculation of gratuity for indefinite contracts may be determined in the referenced Federal Law No. (8) of 1980.

Chapter-II
Applicability

As per Article 3 of the Law, it shall apply to all Establishments, Employers, and workers in the Private Sector in the UAE.

The same will also apply to free region zones that do not have their own labour laws. This Law does not apply to employment relations in the Dubai International Financial Centre and the Abu Dhabi Global Market, considering they have their own labour law regime.

Exemption has been given to the below categories of employers and employees:

a) Employees of federal and local government entities.

b) Members of the armed forces, police, and security.

c) Domestic workers.

Main Definitions

State: United Arab Emirates

Ministry: Ministry of Human Resources and Emiratisation.

Minister: Minister of Human Resources and Emiratisation.

Private Sector: Companies, institutions, establishments, or any other entities wholly owned by individuals or in partnership with federal or local government. Companies and institutions wholly owned by the federal or local government, unless the laws of their establishment stipulate that they shall be subject to the provisions of another law. Establishment: Every economic, technical, industrial, commercial unit, or other categories approved in the State, employing workers and aiming at producing goods, marketing them, or providing services and licensed by the competent authorities.

Employer: Every natural or legal person who employs one or more workers in return for a wage.

Worker: Every natural person authorised by the Ministry to work for one of the licensed establishments in the State, under the supervision and direction of the employer.

Juvenile: Every person who has reached fifteen years old, but has not yet exceeded eighteen years old.

Work: Every human, intellectual, technical, or physical effort performed according to different types of work.

Work Permit: A document issued by the Ministry, according to which a natural person is allowed to work for the licensed establishment.

Employment Contract: Every agreement concluded between the employer and worker, under which the latter is committed to working for the service of the employer and under its supervision and guidance, in consideration of a wage payable by the employer, in accordance with the standard contract forms defined by the Implementing Regulation hereof.

Probationary Period: The period that may be required by the employer, which enables the latter to evaluate the performance of the worker and allows the worker to become familiar with his job duties and the work environment, according to which, the employment contract is either continued or terminated as per the provisions hereof.

Notice Period: The notice period specified in the employment contract requires both parties to the contract to abide by it if either of them wishes to terminate the employment contract.

Basic Wage: The wage stipulated in the employment contract, which is paid to the worker in consideration of his work under the employment contract, on a monthly, weekly, daily, hourly, or piecework basis, and which does not include any other allowances or benefits in-kind.

Wage: The basic wage, in addition to the cash allowances and benefits in-kind allocated to the worker under the employment contract or this Decree Law, and which may include benefits in-kind that the employer shall grant to the worker or their cash equivalent if allocated as part of the wage in the employment contract or the establishment's by-laws; the allowances that the worker is entitled to obtain in return for his effort, the risks he is exposed to while performing his work or for any other reasons; or the allowances granted to meet the cost of living, a percentage of sales, or a percentage of the profits paid for what the worker markets, produces, or collects.

Working Day: The official working day is defined by the implementing resolutions of this Decree Law.

Workplace: The work location agreed-upon in the employment contract, or where the worker undertakes the agreed tasks and services for the employer.

Continuous Service: Uninterrupted service with the same employer or its legal successor from the date of commencement of work.

Day Worker: Each worker receiving a daily wage.

Work Injury: Being exposed to one of the occupational diseases specified in the table issued by a resolution of the Cabinet, or any other injuries arising therefrom, due to or occurring in the course of work. Any injury should be considered a work injury if it is proven that the accident happened to the worker during the period of his commute to and from work, without interruption or deviation from the normal route.

Medical Entity: Any federal or local government entity concerned with health affairs, or any private health establishment licensed to provide health services in the State.

Worker's Family: Spouse, sons, and daughters.

Individual Labour Disputes: Every dispute arising between an employer and a worker alone, whose subject is related to this Decree Law, its Implementing Regulation, and the resolutions issued for its implementation.

Collective Labour Disputes: Every dispute arising between an employer and its workers, whose subject is related to a common interest of all workers or a group of them.

Objective of the Act

The main objective of this new law is defined under Article 2 of this decree law.

As per ARTICLE (2), the objective of this new law shall be as below:

1. Ensure the efficiency of the labour market in the UAE, which contributes to the **attraction and retention** of the best future talents and skills, provides an attractive business environment for employers, and helps both parties to participate in pursuing the UAE' s national development goals.

2. **Regulate the labour relations**, and determine the respective rights and obligations of the parties to this legal relationship in a balanced way.

3. Enhance **flexibility and sustainability** of the UAE's labour market by ensuring the protection of the parties to, development of, and exceptional circumstances encountered by, the work relationship that would have an impact thereon.

4. **support and rehabilitate capacities and skills** of workers in the private sector, in such a way as to promote manpower' s efficiency and productivity in the UAE' s labour market.

5. **Provide protection for both parties** to the work relationship and enable them to obtain their rights within this Decree Law.

So the main objective of this act is **attraction and retention** of talents and provides an attractive business environment; **Regulation of** the labour relations; **flexibility and sustainability** of the labour market; **support and rehabilitation capacities and skills** of workers; and **provide protection** to both employer and employee.

The other change brought by this act is to introduce equality and non-discrimination. The purpose is to align with the best practices and, as per recommendations of ILO. **Article 4** deals with the provisions of Equality, which are as follows:

1. It shall be prohibited to discriminate against persons on the ground of race, colour, sex, religion, national origin, ethnic origin, or disability, in such a way as to weaken equal opportunities or impair equal access to, or continuation of, or enjoyment of rights associated with, employment. An Employer shall not discriminate in respect of works involving the same job duties.

2. Rules and procedures that would enhance the contribution of UAE citizens in the labour market shall not be regarded as discrimination.

3. Without prejudice to the rights prescribed for female workers under this Decree Law, female workers shall be subject to all provisions regulating employment of workers without any discrimination.

4. Women shall receive the same wage as men for the same work, or for work of equal value. Procedures, controls, and standards

for assessment of work of equal value shall be established by decision of the Cabinet, upon the proposal of the Minister.

Important Point:

1. Positive discrimination in favour of Emiratis is permitted.

2. Under the category of grounds of non-discrimination, political opinion is not covered.

3. The concept of Equal pay for equal work is included. A specific legislation shall be issued therewith.

Chapter-III
Recruitment And Employment of Workers

Article 6 of Decree Law deals with the recruitment and employment of workers in the UAE. As per this Article,

a) No work may be performed in the UAE without obtaining a work permit from the Ministry, in accordance with the provisions of this Decree Law and its executive regulations; and

b) No worker may be recruited or employed by any Employer without obtaining a work permit from the Ministry in accordance with the provisions of this Decree Law and its Executive Regulations.

So, neither an employee can work without obtaining a work permit, nor can the employer employ any employee without getting a work permit.

Article 6 of the Executive Regulation specifies the types of work permit that can be issued. The following work permit can only be issued to facilities registered in the Ministry.

S. No.	Type of Work Permit	Purpose of Work Permit
	Work Permit (recruiting a worker from outside the country):	To bring in workers from outside the country.
	Transfer Work Permit	To transfer non-national workers to and from a facility.
	Permit for those who are registered under the residency of their relatives:	It is the permit under which those who are registered under the residency of their relatives are employed to work in a facility.

S. No.	Type of Work Permit	Purpose of Work Permit
	Temporary Work Permit:	for a job whose nature of execution or completion requires a specified period in one of the facilities,
	Task Work Permit:	to recruit a worker from abroad to complete a temporary work or a specific project with a fixed term.
	Partial Work Permit:	- to employ a worker under a part-time contract so that his working hours are fewer than those of his full-time counterparts, - The worker can work for more than one employer after obtaining a permit from the Ministry.
	Juvenile Work Permit:	It is the permit to employ a person who has reached the age of 15 years and has not exceeded 18 years of age.
	Student Training and Employment Permit:	to train or employ a student in the country who has reached the age of 15 years, in accordance with specific controls and conditions, which include a commensurate training and work environment.
	Work Permit for a citizen/person from the Cooperation Council Countries:	to employ citizens or the citizens of the Cooperation Council for the Arab States of the Gulf.
	Work Permit for Golden Residency Holders:	to employ a worker within the country who is a holder of golden residency.
	Work Permit for a Trainee Citizen:	to train a citizen pursuant to his approved scientific qualification.
	Self-Employment Permit	**As described below**

There is one work permit which shall be issued to an individual. It is called Self-Employment Permit. This permit is granted to individuals wishing to engage in self-employment independently (on their self-residency for foreign individuals). By getting this permit, the individual can earn direct income through

- providing services for a specific period of time, or

- performing a task, or

- providing a specific service.

The aforementioned services and/or tasks may be provided to individuals or facilities.

Following are the conditions for issuing this Permit.

- For this permit, sponsorship by a specific employer or body is not required.

- There is no requirement of a valid employment contract,

- and so that this natural person is not, in any way, an employee of these individuals or facilities.

Article 8 of the Executive Regulation further describes self-employment

1. Self-employment is a system for independent and flexible work through which a natural person achieves a direct income by providing their services for a specified period of time, to perform a task, or provide a specific service, whether for individuals or facilities.

2. The Cabinet shall, upon the proposal of the Minister, issue the necessary decisions to determine the procedures, controls, and mechanisms for registering self-employed persons in the Ministry's systems and obtaining, renewing, and cancelling work

permits, in a manner that ensures enhancing the flexibility and requirements of the labour market.

Minister may create new work permits by a decision in accordance with the provisions of the Decree Law.

Article 7 of the Executive Regulation provides for conditions, controls, and procedures for issuing, renewing, and cancelling work permits

1. Conditions for issuing work permits:

- The minimum age for getting a work permit is 18 years. However, there is an exception for the juvenile work permit and the student's training or employment permit.

- Facility applying for the work permit should have a valid licence, and there should be no violations that would lead to the suspension of its activity in accordance with legal regulations.

- The legally authorised signatory of the facility shall only apply for the issuance of the permit on behalf of the facility.

- With respect to the work permit for specialised professions, or the job that requires obtaining a licence to practice the profession, conditions as stipulated in the legislation must be fulfilled and complied with.

- The profession in which the worker will occupy at the employer must be consistent with the activity of the facility.

Facility also needs to comply with any other conditions stipulated by a decision from the Minister or his authorised representative.

2. Procedures for renewing work permits:

A facility that is applying for the renewal of a work permit should follow the following procedures:

- Submit an application pursuant to the channels specified by the Ministry.

- Fulfil the conditions required for issuance.

- Fulfil the required documents, papers and academic qualifications.

- Pay the prescribed fees pursuant to the type of permit and the category of the facility, in accordance with the approved facilities system.

- Any other procedures issued by a decision of the Minister or his authorised representative.

3. Procedures for cancelling work permits:

A facility that is applying for the cancellation of a work permit should follow the following procedure:

- Submit an application to cancel the work permit through the channels specified by the Ministry.

- Complete the required data and attachments.

- Pay the fines for delaying the issuance of the work permit or not renewing it, if any.

- The establishment's acknowledgement that the worker has received his entitlements.

- Any other conditions issued by a decision of the Minister or his authorised representative.

The Ministry may refrain from issuing work permits, renewing them, or it may cancel them and take the necessary legal measures.

If It Is Proven That Facility:

- Has submitted any incorrect documents.

- Is fictitious and does not practise its activity.

- Is non-compliant with the wage protection system or any other systems applied to regulate the labour market in the country.

Any other cases in which a decision is issued by the Minister or his authorised representative.

ARTICLE 5 of the decree law and Article 4 of the Executive Regulation deal with the EMPLOYMENT OF JUVENILES

Article 5 of the Decree Law provides as follows:

1. It shall be prohibited to employ any person who has not attained the age of 15.

2. A Juvenile's employment is conditional upon the following:

   a) A written consent form from the juvenile's parent or guardian is required.

   b) A certificate of medical fitness for the required work issued by the medical institution.

   c) The actual hours of work shall not exceed 6 (six) hours a day and shall be interrupted by one or more breaks, which shall amount in aggregate to one hour. Such break(s) shall be arranged so that no juvenile shall work for more than 4 (four) consecutive hours.

   d) A Juvenile may not be asked to work from 7 PM to 7 AM.

As per Article 4 of the executive Regulation:

1. It is prohibited to employ juveniles in the following jobs and professions:

    a) Dangerous or harmful works and industries.

    b) Professions which are likely to endanger the health or safety of juveniles, due to the nature of the profession or the circumstances in which it is performed.

2. A decision by the Minister, after coordination with the concerned authorities, shall determine the dangerous or arduous works, or the works that, by their nature, cause harm to the health, safety, or morals of the juvenile.

3. The employer who employs the juvenile shall abide by the following procedures:

    a) Maintain a special record of juveniles, which shall include the name of the juvenile, their age, the full name of the person who has guardianship or custody over them, contact details with them, the place of residence of the juvenile, and who has guardianship over them, the date of their employment, and the work in which they are used.

    b) Obtain insurance for the juveniles in the same way as ordinary workers.

    c) Train his juveniles on how to use the means of occupational safety and health.

    d) Place, in an apparent place in the worksite, the provisions of the employment of juveniles.

4. Charitable, educational, and training institutions, and other bodies that aim to rehabilitate or vocationally train juveniles, are exempted from some provisions of Article No. (5) of the Decree Law and the provisions of this Article in accordance with the following controls:

a) The institution must be registered with the relevant government agencies in this description.

b Its actual and registered aim shall be rehabilitation or vocational training, charitable or educational work, or voluntary work.

Important Points:

1. juveniles shall not be employed before reaching the age of fifteen.

2. Written consent of parent or guardian and Medical fitness certificate are important for being eligible for appointment

3. Actual work hours of Juveniles shall not exceed six hour per day, and shall include a break that shall not be less than one hour in total.

4. Juveniles shall not work for more than four consecutive hours.

Employment Agencies, Recruitment Agencies

Article 6 of the Decree Law and Article 9 of the Executive Regulation deal with the requirement of a licence and the conditions and procedures for its issuance.

A licence from the Ministry is compulsory for practising recruitment activities, or mediate in recruiting or employing workers. Without a licence, no one can open a recruitment agency or provide recruitment services.

Executive Regulation 9 specified conditions and procedures for getting the licence.

Employment agency is defined as: "Subject to the provisions of Article No. (6) of the Decree Law, the practice of any of the mediation, temporary employment, and outsourcing work (individually or collectively) shall be deemed the practice of the activity of employment agencies."

The following definitions shall be used within the scope of employment agencies:

a. **Mediation**: It is to bring the views of the two parties to the business together and who represents them, to negotiate on their behalf the terms of the contract, and to be hired for the purpose of establishing a working relationship without the agency becoming a party to it.

b. **Temporary employment and outsourcing**: the use of the worker with the intention of making him available to a third party, and the worker's relationship becomes a direct relationship with the agency that outsourced his services to a third party (the beneficiary).

c. **Beneficiary**: Any natural or legal person with whom the worker is assigned under his supervision, whether for a specific period of time or to perform a task or provide a specific service in accordance with the temporary employment and outsourcing system.

d. **Agency**: Any sole proprietorship or with a legal personality that engages in an activity related to mediation or temporary employment and outsourcing to provide the services of one or more workers for a specified period of time or to perform a task or provide a specific service to the beneficiary.

Conditions for Licence Issuance:

The following conditions must be met in order to obtain a licence to practise any of the agency's businesses:

a) The person in the sole proprietorship or any of the partners in the legal person

- Must not be convicted of a crime involving breach of honour and trust.

- Must not be convicted of a crime involving human trafficking, or of a crime of human trafficking.

- Must not be convicted of a crime involving any of the crimes stipulated in the Decree Law.

There is **some relief** provided by the executive regulation. It says that:

- If the person has been rehabilitated, if he was sentenced to a custodial penalty, or after **the lapse of one year** from the date of the ruling if the **ruling was just a fine**, then he can provide employment agency services.

b) **Bank Guarantee**

1. Licence for a mediation agency: A bank guarantee of not less than (AED 300,000), three hundred thousand dirhams, is required. It shall be submitted to the Ministry. This bank guarantee shall be in force at all times during the validity of the licence.

2. Licence for a temporary employment and outsourcing agency: a bank guarantee of not less than one million dirhams is required.

In both the cases above, a licence must be automatically renewed or provide an insurance system as an alternative to the guarantee.

The Ministry may allocate all or some of the guarantee or insurance to pay any amounts due from the agency for its failure to implement its obligations or for non-compliance with the instructions and decisions issued pursuant thereto.

C) Credit report

A credit report of the licence applicant, or the person in the sole proprietorship, and the partners in the legal person must be submitted. The credit report must be issued by the competent authority.

D) Any other conditions issued by a decision of the Minister.

Procedure of Issuing Licence:

1. Procedures for issuing temporary employment, outsourcing, or mediation agency licences:

   a) An application must be submitted through the channels specified by the Ministry.

   b) The conditions required for the issuance of the licence must be met.

   c) The required guarantees and insurances must be fulfilled.

   d) The prescribed fees must be paid.

   e) Any other procedures issued by a decision of the Minister or his authorised representative.

Renewable:

The licence issued by the Ministry to employment agencies shall be **renewed annually**, provided that it is ensured that all conditions required for licensing are constantly met.

Suspension or Revocation

Procedures for suspending or revoking the licence of employment agencies:

The Ministry may suspend the agency's licence temporarily or cancel its licence if one of the following cases is verified:

a) Absence of one of the conditions on which the licence was issued.

b) If any of the documents or data submitted for licensing purposes are proven to be incorrect.

c) If the agency commits any act that involves some form of forced labour or human trafficking.

d) Non-payment of worker's wages.

e) Violation of any of the other conditions determined by the Ministry.

Control on Employment Agencies:

Temporary employment/outsourcing activity shall:

a) Not provide workers to a beneficiary if the beneficiary company is administratively suspended by the Ministry for committing violations related to the application of the decree law and this resolution.

b) Not provide workers to another agency that engages in temporary employment activity with the aim of employing them with the beneficiary.

c) The person in the sole proprietorship or any of the partners in the legal person must be responsible for applying the provisions of the decree law and its executive regulations to the workers registered with it, informing the competent authorities in the Ministry in the event of his knowledge of any violation or infringement of the rights, health, and safety of workers by the beneficiary.

d) Any other controls decided by the Ministry.

2. To ensure the governance of the relationship between the beneficiary and the worker registered with an employment agency, a contract must be concluded with the beneficiary.

Note:

- An Employer shall not charge the worker or collect from him, recruitment, and employment costs, either directly or indirectly.

- The Minister shall, after coordination with the concerned entities in the UAE, issue the decisions regulating Works in respect of which it is prohibited to recruit and employ workers, and the requirements thereof.

Employment, Work Model, and Type of Contract

Under this new labour law, a major change from the old law has been introduced with respect to the model of work. The model of work shall determine the type of contract to be issued to employees.

Model of Work

Article 7 has dealt with the **model of work** in detail. According to this Article, the following are the main new work models in the UAE.

S. No	Model of Work	Description
1	Full-time employment.	Employee shall be working for one Employer for the full hours of work throughout the Working Days. Employee cannot work for any other employer under this work model.
	Part- time Work	Employees shall be allowed to work for one or more Employers for a specific number of working hours or Working Days. They shall be entitled to prorated Annual leave.
	Temporary Work	An employee may be hired under this model for work that is carried out within a specific period of time, or that involves a specific task and ends with its completion.
	Flexible Work	a work which involves changing working hours or Working Days, depending on the workflow and economic and operational changes of the Employer. The worker may work for an Employer at flexible working hours, depending on the circumstances and requirements of work.

Article (5) of the executive regulation further mentioned the labour pattern in addition to the above-mentioned labour patterns.

	Remote work	All or part of the work is performed outside the workplace, and the communication between the worker and the employer shall be electronic, instead of being physically present, whether the work is part-time or full-time.
	Job sharing	where tasks and duties are divided between more than one worker to perform the tasks agreed-upon in advance, and this division is reflected in the value of the wage due to each of them, making it pro-rata. They shall be dealt with pursuant to part-time controls.

The Ministry may create other work patterns as required by the requirements of the labour market. Subject to what is stipulated in the Decree Law and executive Resolution, both the worker and the employer shall abide by the terms stipulated in the employment contract, in accordance with each pattern of work mentioned in this Article.

TYPE OF CONTRACT:

The contract between the worker and the employer shall be on the agreed-upon pattern of work, in accordance with the contract forms in the Ministry's system, which are:

a) Full-time employment contract.

b) Part-time employment contract.

c) Temporary employment contract.

d) Flexible employment contract.

e) Remote employment contract.

f) Job sharing contract.

g) Any other employment contract forms issued by a decision of the Minister in accordance with the labour classification approved by the Cabinet and work patterns.

The Type of contract depends on the type of model of work. The contract shall be issued in the forms as described by the Ministry.

As per Article (10) of the Executive Regulation, the employment contract shall basically contain:

a) The name and address of the employer.

b) The worker's name, nationality, date of birth and

c) What is necessary to prove his identity, qualification, job, or profession.

d) The Date of joining work.

e) Place of work.

f) Working hours, rest days and,

g) Probationary period, if any.

h) The duration of the contract.

i) The agreed wage, including benefits and allowances.

j) The period of accrued annual leave.

k) The period of warning, the procedures for terminating the employment contract, and

l) Any other data determined by the Ministry in accordance with what is required to regulate the relationship between the two parties.

The flexibility has been given to the worker and the employer to introduce new clauses to the approved contract forms. However, the new clauses should be as per the provisions of the decree law, this resolution and the legal regulations.

The employment contract shall be made in duplicate, one copy to be given to the Employer and the other to the worker.

Can a worker be employed by the employer via an oral contract?

As per labour law requirements, it seems that oral contracts are not permissible. A work permit shall only be issued if there is a written contract between the employer and the worker.

Change in Work Pattern:

The contract may be changed from one work pattern to another, provided that:

a) Both the worker and the employer approve the same.

b) All the dues arising from the first contract must be fulfilled.

c) The procedures set by the Ministry are followed.

When a contract is extended or renewed, a new visa is issued, and the contract is treated as having been renewed on the same terms and conditions, just as it is currently when renewing an unlimited contract.

LIMITED PERIOD employment contract

As per Article 8 of the Decree law, only the limited period employment contract is allowed. Now, the employer cannot issue an unlimited period of contract. The unlimited employment contract has been withdrawn.

Maximum Time Limit of a Contract

The maximum time limit of a limited period employment contract is 3 years. It can be extended or renewed for a similar 3 years or less than 3 years. There is no restriction on how many times an employment contract may be renewed or extended. Therefore, the Employer can extend an employee's contract as many times as they want.

However, this provision has been changed, and there is no minimum limit for the contract duration.

Automatic Extension

If an employee continues to work after the expiry of the initial period and no new contract for renewal or extension has been signed, then it shall be deemed that the employment contract has been extended on the same terms and conditions.

Continuity of Service

The extended contract or renewed contract shall be treated as continuity of service. At the time of calculating the period of continuous service, the total employment period shall be taken into consideration, meaning the initial period plus all extended and renewed periods shall be added for counting continuous period of service.

The Executive Regulations of this Decree Law shall determine the templates of employment contract according to the approved skill levels and the provisions of change of contract from one model to another, and the registration thereof in the Ministry. The employment contract shall be made in duplicate, one copy to be given to the Employer and the other to the worker.

Time Period for Compliance with New Contract Guidelines

All current unlimited contracts need to be converted to limited contracts within one year. Employers have a grace period until 1st February 2023 to convert unlimited term contracts to fixed term contracts compliant with the amended terms.

Main Point:

1. When the contract is renewed or extended after the expiry date of the contract, which is after the 2nd of February 2022, it must be issued in the new contract format and must be for a fixed term.

2. There is no maximum limit set for a limited period contract.

3. The extended term shall be considered an extension of the original term and comprehensive and does not affect the previous terms in accordance with the Law.

Termination of employment contract

If any party terminates the employment contract without complying with the provisions of this Article, they shall pay to the other party a compensation equal to the worker's wage due for the notice period, or the remainder thereof.

A foreign worker who leaves the UAE without complying with the provisions shall not be granted a work permit to work in the UAE for a period of one year from the date of his departure.

The Ministry may exempt certain job categories, skills, and manpower from the non-grant of work permit stipulated above, in accordance with the control and procedure set by the executive regulation of this Decree law.

CHANGE OF EMPLOYMENT:

Under this law, there are a few articles that contain provisions in case a worker changes employment. The following are those provisions:

1. CONTINUITY OF EMPLOYMENT CONTRACTS (Article 48 of decree law)

Employment Contracts, which are valid at the time of a change in the form or legal position of the Establishment, shall continue in force.

The new Employer shall implement the terms of such contracts, the provisions of this Decree Law, its Executive Regulations, and implementing resolutions from the date of the amendment of the Establishment's details with the competent entities.

2. WORKER'S MOVEMENT TO ANOTHER EMPLOYER AFTER EXPIRY OF EMPLOYMENT CONTRACT (Article 49)

A worker may, in the case of the end of the employment contract pursuant to the provisions of this Decree Law, move on to another Employer pursuant to the conditions and procedures set by Article 27 of the Executive Regulations of this Decree Law

Article 27 of the executive regulation has set out the procedures for such movement of workers, which are as follows.

1. In the event of the termination of the employment contract in accordance with the provisions of the Decree Law and this Resolution, the worker may move to work for another employer in accordance with the following conditions and cases:

   a) If the term of the contract agreed-upon between the two parties has expired and has not been renewed.

   b) If the contract is terminated during its validity in accordance with Article No. (42) and Article No. (45) of the Decree Law.

   c) If the employer terminates the contract without reason from the worker.

The Minister may issue a decision specifying the mechanisms for transferring the worker specified in this article.

UNAUTHORISED ABSENCE FROM WORK (Article 50)

There are provisions in the law to punish a worker in case he is absent from work without due authorisation.

A foreign worker shall not be granted a work permit to join any employer in the UAE in the following circumstances.

1. A foreign worker is absent from work illegally.

2. The period of absence is more than 7 consecutive days.

3. This illegal absence is before the expiration of the employment contract.

4. Such illegal absence is without the employer's knowledge of the worker's location or the possibility of communicating with him.

In the above-mentioned circumstance, a foreign worker shall not be granted **another work permit to join another employer in the UAE, for a term of (1) one year** from the date of absence from work.

There is an obligation on the employer as well. If the employer is aware of such absence, they should not employ or keep the individual in their service during that period.

The Employer shall report to the Ministry the absence from work, according to the procedures set by the Article 28 Executive Regulations of this Decree Law.

Exemption from this Article

As per **Article (28) of the Executive Regulations, there are a few exemptions given for not granting a work permit for the period of one year from the date of discontinuation of work. The following are the exceptions:**

a) The worker who is dependent on the residence of his relatives.

b) A worker requesting a new work permit for the same facility.

c) The worker who is of professional skill, or knowledge levels that the country needs.

d) Golden residency holders.

e) Any occupational categories, according to the needs of the labour market in the country, for which a decision is issued by the Minister in accordance with the classification of labour approved by the Cabinet.

The Ministry may exempt certain job categories, skill levels, or manpower from the condition of absence, in accordance with the controls and procedures set by the Executive Regulations of this Decree Law.

<table>
<tr><td align="center">Important Point:</td></tr>
<tr><td>- The previous employer shall not be responsible, but the new employer shall be responsible for all legal obligations.</td></tr>
<tr><td>- The period of the ban begins for one year as of the decision on the application to be absent.</td></tr>
</table>

Chapter-IV

Obligation of The Employer

Article 13 of the decree law puts an obligation on the employer to comply with a few conditions.

Below Are Such Conditions.

The Employer shall:

1. Maintain worker files and records for a minimum period **of 2 years following the date of end-of-service of the worker**. Such files and records of the worker shall be kept as per the conditions, controls, and procedures issued by the decision of the Ministry. The employer must keep worker files and records for a period of at least 2 years from the date of his last working date.

2. Not seize the official documents of the worker after the end of the work relationship. Further, the employer shall not force worker to leave UAE after the end of the work relationship.

3. The Employer shall put in place internal work regulations, including work instructions, sanctions, promotions, benefits, and other by-laws and internal regulations pursuant to the controls set by the Executive Regulations of this Decree Law.

Executive Regulation 14 describes various controls for work instructions, penalties, promotions, rewards, and procedures for terminating the working relationship. According to these regulations, facilities employing more than 50 workers should set regulations to organise work, such as a list of work instructions, penalties, promotions, rewards, and procedures for terminating the working relationship, taking into account the following controls:

a) Organisations should develop regulations in a manner that does not contradict the provisions and rules stipulated in the Decree Law, the provisions of this Resolution, and the legal regulations.

b) Organisations must specify the penalties that may be imposed on violating workers, and the terms and conditions for their imposition.

c) Organisation must prepare work instructions, which should include daily working hours, weekly holidays, festive holidays, and the necessary measures and precautions to be taken into account to avoid work injuries and fire hazards.

d) The list of promotions and rewards must include the criteria and controls for promotions and rewards.

e) The employer must inform the worker of the regulations stipulated in this article by any available means and make him aware of them in the language he understands.

4. The employer shall provide an appropriate e accommodation to worker. Such accommodation must be licensed by the competent entities in accordance with the rules, conditions, and standards applicable in the UAE. Alternatively, the employer may pay him a housing allowance in cash or include the same in the wage.

5. The employer must invest in developing skills of his workers, and procure the minimum training and empowerment tools and programmes according to the provisions of this Decree Law and its Executive Regulations.

6. The Employer must provide the necessary means of protection for workers to protect them from the risks of work injuries and

occupational diseases that can occur at work. Employer must ensure the provision of advice and guidance regulations, and must provide the appropriate training for workers to avoid such risks. The employer must undertake a periodic assessment to ensure that all parties to the Work observe the security and safety requirements, in accordance with the provisions of this Decree Law and its Executive Regulations.

7. The employer should ensure that the worker is aware of his rights and obligations at work, using the means and methods appropriate to the nature of work and workers.

8. The employer shall bear healthcare costs in accordance with the legislation in force in the UAE.

9. The employer shall bear the costs of insurances, contributions, and securities specified by the legislation in force.

10. The employer shall not allow the worker to be employed by others, unless in compliance with the provisions of this Decree Law.

11. The employer shall provide the worker, free of cost, an end-of-service certificate at the expiry of the employment contract. The following should be mentioned in the end-of-service certificate:

    a) The service commencement and end dates.

    b) The total period of service,

    c) The position or the nature of work performed,

    d) The last wage and

    e) The cause of the end of the employment contract.

    Certificate, does not include anything which might harm the reputation of the worker or reduce his opportunities of finding a job. This certificate may be issued at the request of the worker and without any fee. This certificate must be issued free of charge.

12. The employer shall bear the cost of the worker's repatriation to his point of hire or to any other point that was mutually agreed-upon. However, if the worker joins another employer, then this obligation will arise on the latter employer. Also, if the employment contract is terminated for reasons attributable to the worker, then the employer is free from this obligation, and the worker shall bear the cost.

13. The employer shall provide a safe and appropriate working environment.

14. The employer shall follow any other obligations as may be prescribed by the provisions of this Decree Law and its Executive Regulations, or by decisions of the Cabinet, or any other legislation in force in the UAE.

ARTICLE (14) FORCED LABOUR PROHIBITED; OTHER PROHIBITIONS

- An Employer may not use any means susceptible of obliging or forcing the worker, or threatening him with any penalty, to work for him.

- An Employer may not force a worker to do work or deliver a service against their will.

- It shall be prohibited to exercise sexual harassment, bullying, or any verbal, physical, or mental violence against the worker by his Employer, manager, or co-workers.

It is interesting to note here that the word used in the first sentence is "MAY" as far as forcing, threatening with a penalty, or compelling to work against his will is concerned, whereas the word "Shall" is used in the case of sexual harassment, bullying, or any verbal, mental, or physical violence.

ARTICLE 15, ENTITLEMENTS OF WORKER UPON DEATH

In the event of the worker's death during employment, the employer shall pay the worker's family any wages or entitlements due to the worker, in addition to the severance pay due to the worker according to the provisions of this Decree Law and its Executive Regulations. Such payment should be made within a period **not exceeding (10) ten days from the date of death** or the date on which the employer becomes aware of the worker's death.

The worker shall designate in writing someone from his family to receive his entitlements in the event of death.

The employer shall bear all costs for processing and transporting the remains of the deceased worker to his home country or place of residence if his family requests so.

The Ministry shall, in coordination with the concerned entities, put in place a mechanism to retain the worker's entitlements in cases where the war and the delivery of such entitlements to his family or assigns is impossible.

ARTICLE (16): OBLIGATIONS OF worker

The Worker shall:

1. Perform the Work himself under the supervision and control of the Employer, or *his* representative, and as specified in the contract, and not assign the Work to any other worker or person.

2. Display good behaviour and conduct, and observe professional honesty and integrity.

3. Maintain the means of production and working tools in his possession and maintain the same by taking the necessary actions to store them at the appropriate places.

4. Keep confidential all information and data acquired by him in the course of his employment, and not divulge business secrets, and return anything in his possession to his Employer at the end-of-service.

5. Not keep in his personal capacity any hard or soft papers or documents in relation to the business secrets without permission of the Employer or his representative.

6. Implement safety and occupational health instructions set by the Establishment in accordance with the legislation in force or the Work regulations and instructions.

7. Work during the approved Working Days and working hours specified in the employment contract, and communicate and respond effectively to complete the Works assigned to him efficiently.

8. Work diligently and constantly to develop his professional job skills and improve his performance level.

9. Not work for others in violation of the provisions of this Decree Law and other relevant legislation, in force.

10. Evacuate the accommodation provided to him by the Employer, within a period not exceeding **(30) thirty days** from the end of his service. However, the worker may stay in the accommodation after the expiration of such period if the Employer agrees thereto, provided that the worker bears the cost of accommodation or as may be agreed-upon in writing with the Employer.

11. Any other obligations set by the provisions of this Decree Law and its Executive Regulations or any other legislation in force in the UAE.

Chapter-V

Probation Period

Article 9 of the Decree law deals with Probation Period. Following are the main provisions of this Article.

The Employer may employ the worker on probation for a period not exceeding (6) six months from the service commencement date.

A worker may not be placed more than once on probation with the same Employer.

Where a worker successfully completes the Probationary Period and continues in employment, the employment contract shall become effective according to its terms, and the probation period shall be calculated as part of his period of service.

Termination of Contract During Probation

A. By Employer:

The Employer may terminate the worker during the Probation period by giving the worker (14) fourteen days prior written notice.

B: By Worker: -

1. For a Change of Employer

A worker may change employer and may move on to another employer in the UAE during the Probationary Period.

He must notify his current employer in writing at least (1) one month before the date on which he intends to terminate the contract.

In this case, the new Employer shall compensate the first Employer for recruitment or contract costs, unless both employers agree otherwise.

2. For Leaving the UAE

A foreign worker wishing to terminate the employment contract during the probationary period in order to leave the UAE shall notify his employer in writing at least (14) fourteen days prior to the date detetermined for termination of the contract.

If the worker wants to return to the UAE and obtains a new Work Permit within (3) three months from the date of his departure, the new Employer shall pay the compensation for recruitment or contract costs to the original employer, unless agreed otherwise by the worker and the original Employer.

Consequences of non-compliance with this Article

-   If either party terminates the employment contract without complying with the provisions of this Article, he shall pay the other a compensation equal to the Worker's Wage due for the notice period, or the remainder thereof

-   A foreign worker who leaves the UAE without complying with the provisions of this Article shall not be granted a Work Permit to work in the **UAE for a period of one year from** the date of his departure.

The Ministry may exempt certain job categories, skill levels, or manpower from the non-grant of Work Permit, stipulated in paragraph above, in accordance with the controls and procedures set by the Executive Regulations of this Decree Law.

Article (11) of the Executive Regulation deals with granting a new work permit after the termination of the employment contract during the probationary period.

Subject to the provisions of Clause No. (4) and Clause No. (6) of Article No. (9) of the Decree-Law, the Ministry may exempt some workers from the condition of not granting a work permit in accordance with the following controls:

1. The worker must be of the skill, professional, or knowledge levels that the country needs.

2. The worker is dependent on the residence of his relatives.

3. Holders of golden residency.

4. Any occupational categories pursuant to the needs of the labour market in the country, for which a decision is issued by the Minister in accordance with the employment classification approved by the Cabinet.

NON-COMPETE CLAUSE (Article 10 of Decree Law and Article 12 of Executive Regulations)

This clause empowers the Employer to protect its trade secret and business interests. There would be a great implication of this clause on the employment and workers in the UAE. This clause provides for the inclusion of a non-compete clause in the employment contract.

Applicability to Class of Worker

This clause can only be applicable to the worker who gets access to the Employer's customers or business secrets due to the performance of work.

Prohibition

Worker shall not compete with, or be engaged in any business which competes with employer in the same Sector after the expiry of the contract.

Such clause shall specify the place, time, and type of Work to the extent necessary to protect the legitimate business interests,. As per Article 12 of the Executive Regulation, the non-compete clause should specify –

1. The geographical scope for the application of the condition.

2. The nature of the work, in such a way that it seriously harms the legitimate interests of the employer.

3. The period of the non-competition, not exceeding 2 years from the expiry of the contract.

Time Limit

Non-competition period, **shall, not exceed (2) two years,** after the expiration of the contract.

Exception

Non-compete clause shall be void in the case of termination of the employment contract by Employer in violation of the provisions hereof or the breach of his legal or contractual obligations.

Time Limit for Filing the Case

An action filed by an Employer for worker' s breach of the provisions of this Article shall not be heard **after the lapse of (1) one year from** the date on which the violation is discovered.

The Executive Regulations, shall prescribe the provisions regulating this Article, the skill levels or positions that may be exempted from the provision of paragraph 1 above, in accordance with the conditions and controls set by the Regulations.

Burden of Proof in Case of Dispute

In the event of a dispute over the non-competition clause and not being settled amicably, the matter shall be referred to the judiciary, and the burden of proving the damage shall fall on the employer.

Non-execution of Non-compete Clause

The non-execution of the non-competition condition stipulated in Article No. (10) of the Decree Law may be agreed on in writing, in accordance with the following conditions:

a) Payment of compensation, not exceeding three months of the worker's wage agreed-upon in the last contract of the previous employer, by the worker or the new employer, and the prior written approval of the previous employer is required to do so.

b) If the contract is terminated during the probationary period.

c) Any occupational categories pursuant to the needs of the labour market in the country for which a decision is issued by the Minister in accordance with the labour classification approved by the Cabinet.

ENTRUSTING CERTAIN EMPLOYER'S WORK TO ANOTHER PARTY

(Article-11)

If an Employer entrusts another Employer with the performance of any of his basic works, or any part thereof, the latter shall be solely liable for all entitlements of workers engaged in such entrusted work in accordance with the provisions of this Decree Law, unless agreed otherwise by the parties.

ASSIGNMENT OF ANOTHER WORK TO THE WORKER (Article 12)

Article 12 provides for the situation where a worker is supposed to do work that is not part of his employment contract.

- A worker may not be assigned another Work which is substantially different from the Work agreed-upon in the employment contract. However, the Employer may assign another work if such an assignment is necessary or aims to avoid an accident or rectify the consequences thereof. Such assignment should be temporary and as specified by the Executive Regulations of this Decree Law.

  As per Article 13 of the executive regulations, the maximum time limit for such an assignment is **90 days per year**. This clause is invoked where the work assigned to the worker is completely different from the nature of his profession or scientific qualification.

- An Employer may, give the worker with a Work that is not agreed-upon in the employment contract. Such work must be given with the written consent of the worker.

- Where the worker is required to perform work that is not agreed-upon in the employment contract, or to change his place of residence, all resulting costs, including the relocation and accommodation costs, shall be borne by the Employer.

Chapter-VI

Compensation

A. Working Hours

Article 17 and 18 of the Decree Law, and Article 15 of the executive regulations, deal with the provisions of working hours.

The maximum ordinary working hours shall be **(8) eight working hours a day or (48) forty-eight working hours a week**.

As per the executive regulation of this decree law, the employer may employ the worker for additional working hours over the normal working hours. Such additional hours shall not exceed two hours per day.

If the work is necessary to prevent the occurrence of a serious loss or a serious accident, or to eliminate or mitigate its effects, then additional working hours may exceed 2 hours per day.

In all cases, the total working hours must not exceed 144 (one hundred and forty-four) hours every 3 (three) weeks.

A worker may not work more than 5 consecutive hours without breaks (one or more). Aggregate breaks shall not be less than one hour. However, such break(s) shall not be calculated for the purpose of the calculation of working hours.

The periods spent by the worker from the place of residence to the workplace shall not be calculated within the working hours. However, as per Article 15 of the executive regulation of this Decree law, in the following cases, the time periods spent by the worker in moving between his place of residence and the place of work shall be counted as part of the working hours:

a) The period the worker spends in the means of transportation in case of bad weather, and responding to the warnings of the National Centre of Meteorology regarding weather changes and fluctuations.

b) The time the worker spends on the means of transportation provided by the employer in the event of a traffic accident or emergency malfunction.

c) If the two parties expressly agree to the same in the contract.

Working hours and breaks in the Establishment shall be regulated by shifts or, for certain categories depending on their nature (such as on-site positions), as per the manpower classification specified in the Executive Regulations of this Decree Law.

If the worker is not a full-time worker, then he cannot be forced to work more than the hours agreed-upon in the employment contract, without his written consent.

The Employer may stipulate specific working hours if the worker wants to perform Work remotely, whether inside or outside the UAE. However, the worker has to seek consent of the employer for working remotely.

For the holy month of Ramadan, as per the Executive regulations of this Decree law, the normal working hours will be reduced by two hours.

The Cabinet may, upon proposal of the Minister and in coordination with the concerned entities, increase or decrease the daily working hours for certain economic sectors or certain categories of workers, in addition to the working times, breaks, and hours when work is prohibited for certain categories of workers, according to the manpower classification set by the Executive Regulations of this Decree Law.

Exception to the Working Hours

Article 15 of the Executive Regulation of this decree law provides the categories of employees on which the provisions of maximum working hours shall not apply.

1. The following categories are excluded from the provisions related to the maximum working hours:

   a) Chairmen of boards of directors and members of these boards.

   b) Persons occupying supervisory positions, if such positions would enable their occupants to enjoy the powers of the employer.

   c) Workers who make up the crew of naval vessels and workers who work at sea, and enjoy special conditions of service due to the nature of their work.

   d) Businesses whose technical nature requires the continuation of work through successive shifts or hours, **provided that the average working hours do not exceed 56 hours per week.**

   e) Preparatory or complementary works that must necessarily be carried out outside the time limits generally established for work in the facility.

The Minister may issue the necessary decisions to specify the works mentioned in this article, in accordance with the needs of the labour market.

Weekly Rest - Article 21

The worker shall be provided at least one day weekly rest day. This rest day shall be a paid day. The rest day shall be provided under the employment contract or internal work regulation. Currently, Friday is not a compulsory rest day.

OVERTIME COMPENSATION (Article 19)

Normal working hours are 48 per week and 8 hours per day. However, sometimes the employer may ask employees to work beyond normal working hours. If employees are asked to work beyond normal working hours, it shall be treated as overtime. There is a limitation on the maximum overtime an employee can work during a day and within every 3 weeks. In a day, an employee cannot work more than 2 hours of overtime. In every consecutive 3 weeks, an employee cannot work more than 144 working hours in total, including overtime.

An employer may set working hours in such a way that the worker gets a day off in a week.

An employer is required to pay **at least 125% of the basic wage** if overtime work is performed in addition to normal working hours.

If the employee is employed for overtime/extra hours during night time (from 10 PM to 4 AM), then he shall be paid **at least 150% of the basic wages**. This is not applicable to the employees who work in shifts.

WEEKEND/PUBLIC HOLIDAY WORK COMPENSATION

Workers may be required to work on weekly rest days or official holidays (Article 28) specified in the employment contract, internal work regulation, or government notification. In such a situation, they shall be compensated with a **substitute rest day** or shall be paid at **least 150% of the basic wages**.

The worker shall not be employed for more than two consecutive rest days, except for the daily workers.

ARTICLE (20)

EXEMPTED CATEGORIES OF WORKERS

The Executive Regulations of this Decree Law shall determine the categories of workers that can be exempted from the provisions relating to working hours stated herein.

WORK & WAGES

As per Article 22, wages shall be paid in **UAE Dirhams** to the employee. However, it can be paid **in another currency** if the parties agree in the employment contract. Amount or type of wage shall be determined in the employment contract. If such amount or type is not determined in the employment contract, the competent court shall determine the same as a labour dispute.

The Employer shall pay his workers their wages in due time, according to the Ministry's approved systems and as per the conditions, controls, and procedures set by the Executive Regulations of this Decree Law.

Article (16) of the Executive Regulations of this Decree Law describes the conditions, control, and procedures as follows:

1. The employer shall pay the wages to his employees on their due dates, in accordance with the following conditions, controls, and procedures:

   a) The wages must be paid on their due dates as agreed-upon in the contract and in accordance with the regulations and standards set by the Ministry.

b) All facilities registered with the Ministry must pay the wages of their employees on the date they are due, through the wages Protection System, or any other systems approved by the Ministry.

c) All facilities must submit all that is required of them to prove payment of the wages of their workers, if requested to do so.

The Ministry is entitled to take all the legal procedures and measures stipulated in the Decree Law, this Resolution and the relevant legal regulations towards the facility in the event of non-payment of the agreed wage.

Wages Should Be Paid in Full

Article 25 of the Act requires that wages be paid in full, except for authorised deductions permitted by the law.

What are Aome of the Permitted Deductions?

The permitted deductions include the following **(Article 25)**. However, If the reasons requiring deduction from salary are multiple, then, deduction may in no event **exceed (50%) fifty percent** of the wage in a single month.

1. Recovery of loans granted to the worker, up to the maximum monthly deduction from the worker's wage stipulated in this Article, after the written consent of the worker, without any interests.

2. Reinstitution of overpayments made to the worker, provided that no more than 20% twenty percent is deducted from the wage.

3. Payments deducted for the calculation of contributions to schemes, pensions, and insurances, pursuant to the legislation in force in the UAE.

4. Worker's, contributions to a provident fund in the Establishment or the loans due to the fund, as approved by the Ministry.

5. Payments towards any social project, privileges, or other services provided by the Employer and agreed by the Ministry, provided that the worker agrees in writing to contribute thereto.

6. Sums deducted from the worker against violations committed under the Establishment's sanctions by-laws approved by the Ministry, up to (5%) five percent of the wage.

7. Debts due as a result of a court order, up to one quarter of the worker's wage, other than the awarded alimony, where it shall be permissible to deduct more than one quarter of the wage. In case of multiple debts, the amounts required to be paid shall be distributed on a priority basis.

8. Amounts necessary for repair of any harm caused by the worker, as a result of his error or violation of Employer's instructions, and resulting in loss or destruction of, or damage to any tools, equipment,, products or material belonging to the Employer, provided that no more than (5) five days are deducted per month, and no amount in excess of this shall be deducted unless with approval of the competent court.

Minimum Wages

Through Article 27, the concept of minimum wages has been introduced. As per Article 27, the Cabinet may, upon proposal of the Minister and after coordination with the concerned entities, issue a decision determining the minimum wage for workers, or any category thereof

METHOD OF CALCULATION OF WAGE FOR PIECEMEAL PAID WORKERS

ARTICLE (23) prescribes the METHOD OF CALCULATION OF WAGE FOR PIECEMEAL PAID WORKERS. According to this clause, the daily wage of piecemeal paid workers shall be calculated based on the average wage received by the worker for the actual days worked within (6) six months preceding the request or action in relation to any matter relating to the wage.

As per Article 24, a worker may be transferred from a monthly paid category to a weekly, daily, or piecemeal paid category if the worker agrees in writing and without prejudice to the rights accrued to the worker during the period of time he was paid on a monthly basis.

As per Article 26, the employer shall enable the worker to perform his work. In case the employer does not allow the worker to perform his duty, the employer has to pay the full wage to the employee.

Article 17 of the Executive Regulations determines the procedures under which the Worker can leave the job if he is not permitted to perform the Work agreed-upon in the employment contract. As per this Article -

1. The employer shall enable the worker to carry out his work; otherwise, the employer shall pay his agreed wage.

2. If the refusal to enable the worker to perform his work is due to circumstances outside the management of the employer, the employer shall inform the worker of the same, with a guarantee of the payment of his wages.

3. If the worker wants to leave work, he shall notify the employer of the same.

The worker has the option to file a labour complaint in accordance with the applicable legal regulations. Upon submitting a complaint, the Ministry may communicate with the employer and give him a grace period to enable the worker to perform his work. If the employer is not responding, then the Ministry may cancel the worker's work permit and allow him to move to another facility without prejudice to his rights with the employer.

FAQ:

Is my employer permitted to deduct some money from my salary without my consent?

Generally, your employer cannot make a deduction without your consent. Normally, an employer must give a written statement to an employee at or before the time at which any payment of wages or salary is made to the employee, in which statutory deductions are included.

Can I make a complaint when there are unlawful deductions from my salary?

Yes. As a worker, you may file a complaint with the Labour Officer if you are aggrieved by any deductions made by the employer.

LEAVES

A. ANNUAL LEAVES

Annual leave is a period of time off work that an employee is entitled to in each year of service. **As per Article 29**, annual leave is 30 days, during which the employee is entitled to full pay. If the worker has not completed one year but has completed 6 months, then he is entitled to avail paid annual leave of 2 days per month.

Carry Forward of the Unutilised Leave

A worker may carry over his annual leave balance or days thereof to the next year. However, this can only be done as per Establishment by-laws and with the consent of the Employer.

The Employer may not prevent the worker from using his accrued annual leave for more than (2) two years, unless the worker wants to carry it over or be paid in lieu of leave, according to the Establishment by-laws and as specified by the Executive Regulations of this Decree Law.

Article (19) of the Executive Regulations of this Decree Law deals with the **Carrying forward of the annual leave or obtaining a cash allowance for it. As per this article,** The worker may carry over a maximum of half of the annual leave for the following year, or he may agree with the employer to grant him a cash alternative in accordance with the wages he receives at the time of his entitlement to the leave.

In the event the worker's service is terminated, a cash allowance shall be paid to him for the balance of his legally due annual leave in accordance with the basic wage.

Leave Days Payment

A worker shall be entitled to be paid for his days of leave if he leaves Work before the use thereof, irrespective of the length thereof, for the period for which he did not use his leave. The worker shall be entitled to the leave pay for the fractions of the year in proportion to the period of service. Leave payment shall be calculated **on the basis of the Basic Wage.**

He shall also be paid for leave for the fractions of the last year of service in the event of the end of this service before the use of his annual leave balance.

Annual Leave for Part-timer

Part-time worker shall be entitled to an annual leave according to the actual hours spent by the worker in the service of the Employer; such period to be determined in the employment contract, as specified by the Executive Regulations of this Decree Law. **Article 18 of the Executive Regulations** of this Decree Law provides for the annual leave for the part-time work pattern.

As per this article, the part-time worker shall be entitled to annual leave in accordance with the actual working hours spent by the worker with the employer, and its duration shall be determined on the basis of the total working hours after converting them to working days. This should be divided by the number of working days in a year and multiplied by the legally prescribed leaves, resulting in a minimum of five working days per year for annual leave. In the calculation of these due leaves, a part of a day shall be deemed a full day, in accordance with the following:

1. The ratio is equal to the ratio of the employee's work on a part-time contract to the employee's work on a full-time contract.

2. The actual working hours are (8) eight working hours per day as a maximum.

3. The number of hours the employee works on a part-time contract equals the number of hours that have been contracted.

4. The arithmetic equation is the number of working hours in the part-time contract of the employee per year divided by the number of working hours in the full-time contract per year, multiplied by 100, equals the ratio.

The Employer may agree to grant the worker a leave from his annual leave balance during the Probationary Period, and the worker reserves his right to compensation for the outstanding annual leave balance if he does not successfully complete the Probationary Period.

The worker shall use his leave in the year of entitlement. The Employer may fix the dates of leave according to the work requirements and in agreement with the worker, or rotate leaves among workers for the smooth progress of work and shall notify the worker of the date of his leave at least (1) one month before the same.

Days off prescribed by law or agreement shall be counted in, and considered as part of the annual leave if they fall within the dates of annual leave, unless the employment contract or the establishment by-laws provide something more beneficial to the worker.

The Executive Regulations, of this Decree Law shall determine the rules, and conditions regulating the leaves and payment thereof.

FAQ:

What Is Annual Leave?

Annual leave is a period of time off work that an employee is entitled to after every 12 consecutive months of service with an employer. **As per Article 29,** annual leave is 30 days, during which the employee is entitled to full pay. If the worker has not completed one year but has completed 6 months, then he is entitled to avail paid annual leave, 2 days per month.

Must I Take It All at One Time?

The worker shall use his leave in the year of entitlement. The Employer may fix the dates of leave according to the work requirements and in agreement with the worker, or rotate leaves among workers for the smooth progress of work and shall notify the worker of the date of his leave at least (1) one month before the same.

Does this include any other holiday or leave days?

Days off prescribed by law or agreement shall be counted in, and considered as part of the annual leave if they fall within the dates of annual leave. An option for not including is provided under law because, as per law, employers and employees may agree on something more beneficial for the worker.

Is 30 days the maximum amount I am allowed?

Generally, the 30 days for annual leave are as per law. However, it can be decided by the employer and employee to have more days of annual leave.

What happens if my employer accumulates or carries forward my leave?

A worker may carry over his annual leave balance or days thereof to the next year. However, this can only be done as per Establishment by-laws and with the consent of the Employer.

The Employer may not prevent the worker from using his accrued annual leave for more than (2) two years, unless the worker wants to carry it over or be paid in lieu of leave. A maximum of half of the annual leave can be carried forward.

At what rate is annual leave paid? Will I get full pay?

An employee is entitled to full pay during annual leave.

Can I get paid an amount of money in substitution for my annual leave?

Annual leave becomes payable only upon termination/resignation or expiration of a contract and if you have accrued a number of leave days. A worker shall be entitled to be paid for his days of leave if he leaves Work before the use thereof, irrespective of the length thereof, for the period for which he did not use his leave. The worker shall be entitled to the leave pay for the fractions of the year in proportion to the period of service. Leave payment shall be calculated on the basis of the basic wage.

He shall also be paid for leave for the fractions of the last year of service in the event of the end of this service before the use of his annual leave balance.

When Do I Forfeit My Annual Leave?

You can accumulate leave or "carry it over" for a maximum period of 2 years. However, the accumulated leave must be taken within 2 years.

Maternity Leave

Article 30 deals with Maternity leave. A female worker shall be entitled to a maternity leave of (60) sixty days. Out of 60 days, the first 45 days of maternity leave shall be with full pay, and the next 15 days of maternity leave shall be with half pay.

A further 45 day's leave can be taken in case of illness occurring to her or her child due to pregnancy or delivery. This extra 45 days leave shall be without pay. The female worker shall provide a medical certificate issued by the Medical Institution to prove such illness. This extra 45 days shall not be counted in the period of service and for calculation for severance pay or subscription to the pension systems.

The maternity leave may be taken after 6 months of pregnancy. This leave can be taken whether the child is stillborn, delivery takes place, or the child is born alive but then dies.

A female worker who delivers a sick child or a child with special needs, whose health condition requires a continuous companion based on a medical report from the Medical Institution, shall be entitled to thirty days leave with full pay commencing from the expiry of the maternity leave, such period to be extended for another thirty days without pay.

The Employer shall grant the female worker a maternity leave when she requests it at any time starting from the last day of the month preceding the month of delivery, as evidenced by a certificate from the Medical Institution.

A female worker obtaining maternity leave or absence from work under this Article shall not lose her right to other leaves.

If a female worker works for another employer during the period of leave stated in this article, her employer may deprive her of her wage for the period of leave, or recover any wages paid to her.

It shall not be permissible to terminate, or give notice to a female worker by reason of pregnancy or for having obtained maternity leave or absence from work pursuant to the provisions of this Article.

A female worker shall be entitled, after reporting back to work from maternity leave and for a period not exceeding (6) months following the date of delivery, to one or two breaks per day to nurse her child, provided that such period does not exceed one hour.

FAQ:

How does an employee become eligible for maternity leave?

A female employee shall be entitled to maternity leave. A female employee who seeks to exercise her right to maternity leave shall, if required by the employer, produce a certificate as to her medical condition from a qualified medical practitioner or midwife.

The aforementioned leave may be taken after 6 months of pregnancy. This leave can be taken whether the child is stillborn, delivery takes place, or the child is born alive but then dies.

How many days of maternity leave is an employee entitled to?

A female worker shall be entitled to a maternity leave of (60) sixty days. Out of 60 days, the first 45 days of maternity leave shall be with full pay, and the next 15 days of maternity leave shall be with half pay.

A further 45 days leave can be taken in case of illness occurring to her or her child due to pregnancy or delivery. This extra 45 days leave shall be without pay. The female worker shall provide a medical certificate issued by the Medical Institution to prove such illness. This extra 45 days shall not be counted in the period of service and for calculation for severance pay or subscription to the pension systems.

Is there any limit on the number of times that an employee can take maternity leave?

No, the law does not set a limit on the number of times maternity leave is availed.

Can the Period of Maternity Leave Be Extended?

Not in terms of extending the maternity leave, but an extension may be granted with the consent of the employer by taking sick leave, annual leave, compassionate leave, or other leave entitlements.

If an employee takes maternity leave, would she still be entitled to full pay?

The first 45 days of maternity leave shall be with full pay, and the next 15 days of maternity leave shall be with half pay.

Can an employer terminate an employee because she is pregnant and on maternity leave, or fire them soon after resuming work from maternity leave for the same reason?

No, an employer shall not dismiss a woman worker because of her absence from work due to maternity leave. No employer shall discriminate, directly or indirectly, against an employee or prospective employee, or harass an employee or prospective employee on grounds of pregnancy.

Can a pregnant woman be allowed to do overtime work?

The law is not specific on requirements for the health protection of pregnant women or new mothers. However, employers have a general duty to ensure the health, safety, and welfare of all workers at their worksite.

Can an employer post a pregnant woman outside her area of residence to work?

No relevant provisions are identified, although it is treated as in the case of overtime work and pregnant women.

Health and Safety: What does the law say when one is pregnant?

The law is not specific on requirements regarding the health protection of pregnant women or new mothers. The Act does not provide any protection for pregnant employees in respect of pollution or hazardous working environments, even though employers have a general duty to ensure the health, safety, and welfare of all workers at their worksite.

Health and Safety: What about breastfeeding according to the law?

After returning from maternity leave, a female worker is entitled to one or two breaks for breastfeeding her child, not exceeding one hour per day.

Working and Kids: Is there allowance for parental care?

The law does not specifically provide for any allowance for parental care, except parental leave for 5 days.

Sick Leave

Article 31 deals with Sick leave. According to this Article, a worker can take sick leave after completion of the probation period. The total sick leave shall not exceed 90 days in respect of each year of service. The first 15 days of sick leave shall be fully paid. The next 30 days of sick leave shall be half paid, and subsequent sick days shall be without pay.

Worker or their representative must report their illness, along with a medical report from a Medical Institution, to their employer within a maximum of 3 working days. Work injury has been excluded from this reporting requirement.

A worker shall not be entitled to any paid sick leave during the Probationary Period. However, the Employer may grant him an unpaid sick leave, based on a medical report issued by the Medical Institution stating that the leave is necessary.

No wage shall be paid for the sick leave if the illness results from the worker's misconduct, according to cases determined by the Executive Regulations of this Decree Law.

The Employer may dismiss the worker if he fails to report to work, after exhausting his sick leave referred to in this Article, and the worker shall reserve all his entitlements pursuant to the provisions of this Decree Law and its Executive Regulations.

As per Article 20 of the Executive Regulations, the worker shall not be paid wages if **sick leave arises from the employee's misconduct. As per this article,** the worker shall not receive a wage during sick leave in the following cases:

a) If the disease is due to the worker's conduct, such as consumption of alcohol or drugs.

b) If the worker violates safety instructions in accordance with the legislation in force in the country, such as instructions for crises and disasters, traffic and traffic regulations, or any safety procedures and controls specified in the facility's by-laws, and the worker was informed of them, acknowledged their understanding, and committed to them.

For the application of what was stated in paragraph (a) of this Article, a report from the concerned authorities in the country is required to prove that the disease resulted from the worker's misconduct.

TERMINATION OF EMPLOYMENT FOR MEDICAL UNFITNESS (Article 46)

The Employer may not terminate the worker for medical unfitness before the worker exhausts all his legal leaves, and any agreement contrary to this shall be void, even if it preceded the entry into force of the provisions of this Decree Law.

FAQ:

Who pays when I am sick, according to the law?

Under the Act, the employer shall provide proper healthcare for his/her employees during serious illness. The employee must notify the employer of their illness in order for this to take place.

Do I, as a worker, get a salary if I am sick?

The total sick leave shall not exceed 90 days in total in respect of each year of service. The first 15 days of sick leave shall be fully paid. The next 30 days of sick leave shall be half paid, and subsequent sick days shall be without pay.

A worker shall not be entitled to any paid sick leave during the Probationary Period. However, the Employer may grant him an unpaid sick leave, based on a medical report issued by the Medical Institution stating that the leave is necessary.

In terms of payment, what happens if I am ill for a long time?

The Employer may dismiss the worker if he fails to report to work, after exhausting his sick leave referred to in this Article, and the worker shall reserve all his entitlements pursuant to the provisions of this Decree Law and its Executive Regulations.

In practice, there is provision for an employee to obtain unpaid leave after paid sick leave. Any employee who is ill should seek and obtain permission from the relevant authority for absence from the workplace due to ill health. Absence from duty without permission is actionable in accordance with Service Regulations.

What happens if the illness is related to my job?

It is the responsibility of the employer to ensure that his/her employees get proper medicines during illness and (if procurable) medical attendance during serious illness. The employer is required to take all reasonable steps to ensure that the illness of an employee is brought to their notice as soon as reasonably practicable after the first occurrence of the sickness. An employer can take out workmen's compensation insurance to meet such claims.

What happens if the illness is related to my gender?

No form of discrimination on the grounds of gender is allowed under law. Women and men have the right to equal treatment, protection, and equal benefit of the law. An employer is required to give equal attention to his/her employee, irrespective of gender.

What does the law say about medical insurance and employees?

An employer is under obligation to provide medical treatment to his/her employees during their time of service and, if possible, medical attendance during serious illness. The employer should take up a medical insurance scheme for the benefit of his/her employees.

OTHER LEAVES: Article 32 of the Decree law and Article 21 of the Executive regulation deal with other types of leaves

A. Bereavement Leave

A worker shall be entitled to paid bereavement leave of (5) five days for the death of the spouse, and (3) three days of bereavement leave for the death of a parent, child, sibling, grandchild, or grandparent, commencing from the date of death.

B. Parental Leave

A worker shall be entitled to a paid parental leave of (5) five Working Days for the worker (father or mother) who has a newly born child, in order to take care of their child. Such leave shall be taken successively or intermittently, during the period of (6) six months following the date of birth of the child.

The worker is entitled to parental leave, provided that he submits evidence of the birth of a child.

C. Study Leave

If a worker has completed 2 years of service with their employer, then a study leave for 10 days per year may be given in order to sit for examinations, if the worker is affiliated with an educational institution.

The worker may be granted study leave to perform the tests, provided that he has obtained an academic acceptance from one of the accredited university institutes or colleges in the country, indicating the type of study, specialisation, and duration of the study. The facility may request proof of the dates of performing the tests.

D. Sabbatical Leave

An Emirati Worker shall be entitled to be paid sabbatical leave for national service, pursuant to the legislation in force in the UAE.

The citizen worker is entitled to a full-time leave to perform the national and reserve service, pursuant to the laws and regulations in force in the country.

Where is this mentioned? Proof shall be submitted from the concerned authorities for leaves referred to in this Article.

The Executive Regulations shall determine the provisions on the grant and regulation of leaves referred to in this Article.

A worker may combine bereavement leave, parental leave, annual leave and unpaid leave.

UNPAID LEAVE

After the consent of the Employer, the worker may take unpaid leave.

Unpaid leave above shall not be counted in the period of service of the worker with the Employer and within the Pension System, according to the relevant legislation in force.

As per Article 34, A Worker who does not report to work after the end of his leave without good cause shall not be entitled to his Wage throughout the period of his absence after the end of leave.

As per Article 35, in case of termination of a contract during a leave period, the notice period of termination, as agreed-upon in the employment contract, shall commence following the date on which the worker returns from leave. However, both parties, with an agreement, may decide otherwise.

Chapter-VII

Health & Safety

Occupational Safety and Care

As per Article 36, the establishment shall observe the provisions of Federal Law (13) 2020 on public health and all its implementing resolutions, and any other legislation in this respect.

The Executive Regulations of this Decree Law shall determine the role of the Ministry and the provisions relating to safety, protection, and healthcare of workers.

Article 22 of the Executive Regulations of this Decree Law deals with the Worker's safety, protection, and health care. As per this Article

1. Every employer shall:

    a) Provide the appropriate means of protection to protect workers from the dangers of occupational injuries and diseases that may occur during working hours, as well as the dangers of fire and all other dangers that may result from the use of machines and other work tools, and follow all other methods of prevention decided by the Ministry in this regard.

    b) Place in a prominent and conspicuous place in the workplace detailed and clear instructions regarding the means of preventing fire and protecting workers from the dangers that they may be exposed to while performing their work, methods of prevention, and how to treat accidents that occur because of such dangers, provided that the instructions are in Arabic and in another language that workers understand when necessary. The employer shall put warning signs in front of the dangerous sites.

c) Shall inform his employees, prior to assuming work, of the risks of the profession they practice, such as the dangers of fire, machinery, falls, occupational diseases and others.

d) Assign a specialist to supervise first aid and to provide medical aid, and all that is necessary for each first aid box.

e) Provide the necessary means to prevent fire, as well as the appropriate extinguishing devices for the materials existing in the facility and the materials used in industries.

f) Take the necessary measures to ensure, on an ongoing basis, that the prevailing conditions in the workplace provide adequate protection for the health and safety of the workers employed in the facility.

g) Take the appropriate scientific means to prevent, reduce, or eliminate health hazards in the workplace.

h) Take the necessary precautions to protect workers from the dangers of falling, falling objects, flying fragments, sharp objects, caustic or hot liquid materials, flammable or explosive materials, or any other materials with a harmful effect. Also, take the necessary precautions to protect workers from the dangers of compressed gases and electricity.

i) Hang guiding signs in the place of machines or the place of various operations indicating the type of necessary technical instructions in Arabic and in another language that the workers understand, when necessary.

2. The worker shall use the protective equipment and the clothes that he is provided with, implement all the instructions of the

employer aimed at protecting from dangers, and refrain from doing any work that would obstruct those instructions.

The worker must abide by the orders and instructions related to safety and work safety precautions, use the means of prevention, and undertake to take care of what is in his possession. It is prohibited for the worker to commit any act that leads to the non-implementation of the aforementioned instructions or to the misuse of the means established to protect the health and safety of workers, or to the harm or destruction of these means.

The employer shall have the right to apply a list of penalties and sanctions for each worker who violates the provisions stipulated in this clause.

3. The Ministry shall coordinate with the authorities related to labour health, occupational care, and safety for workers, pursuant to the following:

    a) To follow up on the employer's commitment to health insurance for workers in accordance with the legislation in force in the country.

    b) To coordinate with the local and federal competent authorities regarding the health and safety of workers.

    c) To continuously verify the standards and requirements set at the federal and local levels related to the health and safety of workers, work injuries, and ensuring the commitments of workers to follow them.

    d) To oversee, inspect and apply administrative penalties to facilities that violate occupational health and safety instructions.

    e) To circulate the decisions issued by the authorities concerned with public health regarding the health and safety of workers.

Compensation of Work Injuries and Occupational Diseases

Work injuries may eventually create permanent partial disability or permanent total disability. **As per Article 37**, the Cabinet, upon the proposal of the Minister and in coordination with the concerned entities, shall decide the amount of compensations, conditions, and procedures to be followed in the event of work injuries, occupational diseases, compensation in case of death, and rules of distribution and amount thereof.

This article further states that if a worker suffers a work injury or occupational disease, the employer shall:

a) Bear the worker's treatment costs until he recovers and reports to duty, or proves his disability, in accordance with the conditions, controls, and procedures set by the Executive Regulations of this Decree Law.

b) If the work injury or the occupational disease prevents the worker from performing his Work, the Employer shall pay the worker his full wage for the period of treatment or for a term of (6) months, whichever is less. If the treatment period exceeds (6) months, the worker shall be paid the half wage for the subsequent period of (6) months or until he recovers or proves his disability or dies, whichever is earlier.

c) If the worker dies as a result of work injury or occupational disease, his family shall be entitled to compensation equal to **the Basic Wage of the Worker for (24) twenty-four months**, provided that the compensation amount is not less than AED 18,000 and not more than AED 200,000. Compensation amount shall be calculated on the basis of the basic wage received by the worker before his death and shall be distributed to his successors as specified by the Executive Regulations of this Decree Law. The family shall reserve the rights to severance pay and any other financial entitlements due to the worker.

Article 23 of the Executive Regulation of this Decree Law deals with work injuries.

1. The employer shall, if the worker suffers any work injury or occupational disease, pay the treatment expenses of the worker in accordance with the following terms and controls:

   a) The worker shall be treated in a governmental or private treatment facility.

   b) The treatment expense shall continue unless the worker is cured or incapacitated.

   c) The treatment shall include hospital stay, surgeries, expenses for x-rays and medical tests, as well as the purchase of medicines and rehabilitation equipment, evaluation of limbs, and prosthetic devices for those who are incapacitated.

   d) The treatment expense includes the transportation expenses required for the worker's treatment.

2. The worker shall abide by the orders and instructions related to work safety and security precautions, and he must use the means of prevention and undertake to take care of what he has of them. It is prohibited for the worker to commit any act that leads to the non-implementation of the aforementioned instructions or to the misuse of the means established to protect the health and safety of workers, or to the harm or destruction of these means.

3. The worker is not entitled to compensation for a work injury if it is proven through the competent authorities that the injury occurred as a result of an intentional violation of the preventive instructions announced in visible places in the workplace, provided that the employer complies with the following controls:

a) To educate the worker about the detailed instructions regarding the means of preventing fire and protecting workers from the dangers they may be exposed to while performing their work, in Arabic and another language that the worker understands, when necessary.

b) To inform the worker before practising the job of the dangers of his profession and obligate him to use the prescribed means of prevention for the same. The employer shall provide appropriate personal protective equipment for workers and train them to use them.

c) To train the worker on the safety methods mentioned in the labour protection instructions.

d) To teach the worker, upon employing him, about the dangers of his profession and the means of protection he must take. The employer must post detailed, written instructions in this regard in the workplace.

4. If a work injury or an occupational disease leads to the death of the worker, the compensation shall be paid to those entitled to it in accordance with the legislation in force in the country, or as determined by the worker prior to his death.

As per Article 38, a Worker shall not be entitled to compensation for work injury, if the investigations of the competent authorities reveal that any of the following events occurred:

1. In case of deliberate self-injury.

2. If injury occurs under the influence of alcohol, drugs, or other psychotropic substances.

3. If the injury is the direct result of a deliberate violation of precautionary instructions posted in visible places at the

Workplace, as specified by the Executive Regulations of this Decree Law.

4. If the injury is the direct result of the worker, 's deliberate misconduct.

5. If the worker refuses, without serious cause, to undergo a check-up or follow the treatment prescribed by the Medical Institution.

Chapter-VIII

Disciplinary Sanction

It is the duty of the worker to follow the provisions of this Decree Law, its Executive Regulations, and Company policies. If the worker fails to follow or disobeys them, then the law provides the option for the employer to take disciplinary action against the worker.

As per Article 39, if a worker violates provisions of this Decree Law, and its Executive Regulations and implementing resolutions, then the employer may take the following action against such a worker

a) Written attention draw.

b) Written warning.

c) Deduction of a **maximum of (5) five days** in a month from the wage.

d) Suspension from work for a period not exceeding 14 (fourteen) days, and denial of wage during suspension.

e) Denial of periodic bonus for a maximum of (1) one year, where Establishments have periodic bonus systems in place, and the worker is entitled thereto pursuant to the provisions of employment contract or the establishment by-laws.

f) For establishments having promotion system in place, denial of promotion for a **maximum of (2) two years.**

g) Dismissal with severance pay.

The Executive Regulations shall determine the conditions, controls, and procedures necessary to impose any of the sanctions referred above, and the relevant grievance mechanism.

Article (24) of The Executive Regulations deals with the **Controls for imposing disciplinary penalties on workers, which are as follows.**

Disciplinary Action:

Worker shall be informed in writing about the offence committed by him. He must be given a chance to defend himself. The employer must investigate his defence. All these proceedings should be recorded in writing in a report and deposited in his private file, indicating the penalty at the end of this report.

The worker must be informed, in writing, of the penalties imposed on him, their type and amount, the reasons for inflicting them, and the penalty he will face in case of repeating the same violation.

When deciding on the imposition of an appropriate penalty in response to the gravity and seriousness of the committed violation, the employer shall take the following criteria into account:

a) Extent of breach of confidentiality of data and information related to work.

b) The impact of the violation on the health and safety of the worker or workers in the facility.

c) The financial impact of the violation.

d) The effect of the violation on the reputation of the facility and its employees as a result of committing the violation.

e) Exploitation of authority entrusted to the violating worker by him.

f) The worker's repetition ratio of all kinds of violations.

g) The existence of a criminal or moral part in the committed violation.

The employer shall draw up a list of penalties, explaining each of the disciplinary penalties set forth in Article No. (39) of the Decree Law.

Time limit for initiating disciplinary action and imposing penalties:

Employers should initiate disciplinary action within 30 days of detecting the issue. The worker may not be accused of a disciplinary violation that has been detected for more than (30) thirty days.

A disciplinary penalty may not be imposed after the date of the end of the investigation of the violation and its confirmation against the worker by more than (60) sixty days.

TEMPORARY SUSPENSION FROM WORK:

-   **Article 40 provides for the temporary suspension from work** during a disciplinary investigation. When a disciplinary investigation is ongoing against a worker, and if it is necessary in the interest of the investigation to suspend that worker, then in that case, the employer may temporarily suspend the worker for a maximum of 30 days. During suspension, such worker shall be paid half wages. After completion of the investigation, if violation is not established, or the worker is sanctioned with just a warning, or the investigation is dismissed, then he should be paid full wages for the suspension period.

-   If a worker is accused of an offence against life, property, honour, or honesty and there is a pending final decision by the competent judicial entity, the Employer may temporarily suspend the worker from work. The worker shall not be eligible for his wages during the suspension period. If the worker is allowed not to go to trial or is acquitted, or the investigation is dismissed for lack of proof, then the worker shall return to work and shall be paid his suspended wages.

Article 41 of the decree law provides that any offence committed by a worker outside the workplace shall be exempted from disciplinary action, unless such act is related to the work.

Only one disciplinary sanction may be imposed in respect of one violation, in accordance with Article (39) hereof.

Worker Rights:

Every employer who employs 50 workers or more must put in a conspicuous place or through any other appropriate mechanism a system for complaints and grievances that workers can access. This system must stipulate that the worker shall have the right to raise their complaint or grievance to the employer or their representative, and that their grievance shall be answered in writing and within a specified period.

- Without prejudice to the worker's right to file a labour complaint, the worker shall have the right to complain to the management of the facility about any penalty imposed on him. The complaint shall be submitted to the facility's management, detailing the appealed penalty. The worker shall not be harmed by submitting his complaint. The employer must inform the worker of the outcome of the complaint.

Chapter-IX

Severance Pay For Full-Time Workers

Article 51 of the decree law deals with the severance pay for the full-time worker in the UAE.

National worker is, entitled to a severance pay at the end of his service pursuant to the legislation regulating pensions and social security in the UAE.

A foreign full-time worker is entitled to a severance pay as per the following conditions.

a) Must have completed one or more years in the Continuous Service.

b) The calculation is divided on the basis of duration in the company, as below.

- For each of the first 5 years of the Service, severance pay shall be calculated for 21 (twenty-one) Working Days, wage for each of the first five years of service.

- For the subsequent year of service after the expiry of the first 5 years of the Service, (30) thirty Working Day's wage for each subsequent year of service.

c) Severance pay shall be calculated on the basis of the **Basic Wage**. The severance pay shall be calculated on the basis of the last basic wage received by the foreign worker, for monthly, weekly, daily paid workers and on the basis of the average daily wage for piecemeal paid workers.

A foreign worker shall be entitled to a severance pay for the fractions of the year in proportion, to the period of service provided, that he has completed one year of continuous service.

Days of absence from work without pay shall not be counted within the period of service.

Maximum Payment Under Severance Pay

The severance pay for a foreign worker shall not exceed, in aggregate, two year's wage.

Deduction from the End-of-service Benefit:

The Employer may deduct from the severance pay any amounts due by law or court order, in accordance with the conditions and procedures set by the Executive Regulations of this Decree Law.

Article 29 of the Executive Regulations of this Decree Law deals with the **Controls for deduction from the end-of-service benefits for workers.**

1. The employer may deduct from the employee's end-of-service benefits any amounts due legally or by judicial ruling, in accordance with the following conditions and procedures:

    a) If the amounts owed by the worker to recover the loans, or the amounts paid to him, are in excess of his right.

    b) To recover the sums that are deducted for the purposes of calculating participation in bonuses, retirement pensions, and insurances, in accordance with the legislation in force in the country.

    c) As amounts deducted from the worker because of the violations he commits in accordance with the penalties regulations in force in the facility and approved by the Ministry.

    d) As debts owed in implementation of a court ruling issued against the worker.

    e) As amounts to repair the damage caused by the worker, as a result of his fault or his violation of the employer's instructions.

2. The employer must have taken the procedures stipulated in the Decree Law and in the executive Resolution in the event that the amounts due are violations committed by the worker or as a result of damages due to his fault, provided that the time passed since the amounts are due from the date of their entitlement is not (3) months, unless it is agreed otherwise.

---

1. End-of-Service Gratuity will be calculated on the basis of working (and not calendar) days.

2. Severance pay shall be calculated on the basis of the last drawn **Basic Wage**.

3. Days of absence from work without pay shall not be counted within the period of service.

4. The severance pay for a foreign worker shall not exceed, in aggregate, two year's wage.

SEVERANCE PAY FOR WORKER EMPLOYED UNDER OTHER WORK MODELS (Art. 52)

Article 52 gives a mandate to the Executive Regulations of this Decree Law to determine the mechanism regulating the severance pay for foreign workers other than full-time work in such a manner that enhances efficiency and attractiveness of the labour market, and as dictated by the interest of the parties to the employment contract.

Accordingly, Article (30) of the Executive Regulations of this Decree Law, **the End-of-service benefits for employees of other work patterns are as below.**

The calculation of the end-of-service benefits for employees with part-time or job sharing patterns, other than the full-time system, shall be pursuant to the following mechanism:

1. The number of working hours in the employment contract per year, divided by the number of working hours in the full-time contract, multiplied by 100, equals the ratio multiplied by the value of the end-of-service benefits of the full-time employment contract.

2. The end-of-service benefits do not apply in the case of temporary employment if their duration is less than one year.

PAYMENT OF WORKER ENTITLEMENTS AFTER THE END OF THE CONTRACT

As per **Article 53** of the Decree Law, the Employer should pay the worker within 14 (fourteen) days after the end of the contract, all his wage and other entitlements provided for in this Decree Law and its implementing resolutions, the contract, or the Establishment by-laws.

FAQ:

What terminal benefits am I entitled to as an employee upon the termination of my employment contract?

- Any remuneration for work done by an employee before termination.

- Any annual leave pay due to an employee.

- Any notice pay due to an employee.

- Any severance pay due if an employee qualifies for this.

- Certificate of Service.

- The employer shall bear the cost of the worker's repatriation to his point of hire or to any other point that was mutually agreed-upon. However if the worker joins another Employer then this obligation will arise on latter employer. Also if the employment contract is terminated for reasons attributable to the worker then also employer is free from this obligation and worker shall bear the cost.

If my contract as an employee is terminated due to misconduct, am I still entitled to severance pay?

Yes, employees are eligible for severance pay even in the case of termination of employment on grounds of misconduct.

Am I, as an employee, entitled to severance pay upon retirement?

Yes, foreign workers are eligible for severance pay even in case of retirement. However, national workers are entitled to other forms of payment, such as a pension fund or social security scheme provided by the government.

How Is Severance Pay Calculated?

a) The calculation is divided on the basis of duration in the company as below:

   - For each of the first 5 years of the Service, severance pay shall be calculated for (21) twenty-one Working Days, wage for each of the first five years of service.

- For the subsequent years of service after the expiry of the first 5 years of service, (30) thirty Working Day's wage for each subsequent year of service.

b) Severance pay shall be calculated on the basis of the Basic wage. The severance pay shall be calculated on the basis of the last basic wage received by the foreign worker, for monthly, weekly, daily paid workers and on the basis of the average daily wage for piecemeal paid workers.

CHAPTER-X

Termination of Employment Contract

Article 42 of Decree Law describes conditions under which an employment contract can be terminated. Under the following events, an agreement can be terminated.

1. An agreement can be terminated by mutual written agreement of the employer and worker.

2. An agreement can be terminated by the efflux of time, which means on expiration of the contract term, unless it is extended or renewed.

3. Upon the will of either party, after giving due notice as agreed in the employment contract, such termination shall be as per the provisions of this Decree Law in relation to termination of the employment contract.

4. In the event of the death of the Employer, the agreement stands terminated.

5. An agreement is also terminated in the event of the worker's death or permanent total disability. There should be a certificate from the Medical Institution to be provided to the employer.

6. If the worker is convicted by a final order to a custodial penalty for a term of not less than (3) three months.

7. The permanent closure of the Establishment, pursuant to the legislation in force in the UAE.

8. If the Employer becomes bankrupt, insolvent or unable to continue in business for any economic or exceptional reasons, in accordance with the conditions, controls and procedures set by the Executive Regulations and the legislation in force in the UAE.

9. If the worker does not meet the conditions for renewal of the Work Permit for any reason outside the control of the employer.

NOTICE OF TERMINATION OF EMPLOYMENT CONTRACT

Article 43 further elaborates on the termination of the contract by giving notice to the other party. Each party has an option to terminate the contract for **"good cause"** by giving the other party a notice of termination.

Notice Period

- notice period shall be decided by contract.

- notice period shall be equal for both parties. However, in the interest of the worker, it may be different also.

- There is no minimum and maximum notice period defined under the Act as it leaves it to parties to decide through contract. However, it states that the worker shall continue to perform his work during the notice period if the notice period is not less than 30 days and not in excess of 90 days.

- Employment contract shall remain in force until the expiry of the notice period.

- Wages shall be paid to the worker for the notice period. Both parties may agree to waive the notice period or shorten it. The worker shall be entitled to **receive his wages for** the complete notice period, irrespective of the shortened notice period.

Breach of notice period

- If any Party breaches the notice period, then it shall pay the other party compensation, called pay in lieu of notice period.

- This compensation shall be equal to the wages of **the worker for the entire notice period, or any remainder thereof.**

- Notice pay shall be calculated based on the last wage received by the worker for monthly, weekly, daily, or hourly paid workers, and on the basis of the average daily wage referred to herein for piecemeal paid workers.

Absence from Work During Notice Period

- If the employment contract is terminated by the Employer, the worker shall be entitled to absence from Work during the notice period for **one working day, "without pay," per week**, to search for another job.

- The Worker may designate the day of absence. They need to notify the employer at least (3) three days before such a planned absence.

<table>
<tr><td colspan="2" align="center">Important points:</td></tr>
<tr><td>1.</td><td>Employers are required to pay all final termination payments to employees within 14 days of the termination date, which will include end-of-service gratuity payable by the employer.</td></tr>
<tr><td>2.</td><td>Within the probationary period, the employer may terminate an employee at any point in time. However, employees are obligated to provide their employer with 14 day's notice if they choose to terminate their employment themselves.</td></tr>
</table>

DISMISSAL OF WORKER BY EMPLOYER WITHOUT NOTICE

Article 44 gives the right to the employer to dismiss the worker without prior notice under certain circumstances.

Dismissal decision shall be,

- In writing and

- with reason of dismissal, and

- must be given to the worker.

Following are the events for which the employer may terminate a worker without notice.

1. If the Worker assumes

   a) False identity, or

   b) submits false certificates or documents.

2. If the worker commits an error resulting in:

   a) Gross material losses to the employer, or

   b) deliberately cause harm to the property of the Employer and admits to the same.

   In this case, the Employer must notify the Ministry of the incident within (7) seven working days of being aware of the occurrence thereof.

3. If the worker violates the by-laws of the Establishment in relation to Work and worker's Safety or the Workplace.

   One condition before taking any action under this clause is that the Employer should ensure that the following two conditions for such instructions are complied with.

   a) In writing and posted in a visible place, and

   b) The worker, has been advised thereof.

4. If the worker fails to perform his main duties in accordance with the employment contract, and a proper investigation has been carried out and at least 2 warnings have been given to remedy such failure, then the employer can dismiss the worker.

5. If the worker divulges the business secrets in relation to industrial or intellectual property, which results in losses to the Employer or loss of opportunity, or a personal benefit for the worker.

6. If the worker is found during working hours in a state of drunkenness or under the influence of a narcotic or psychotic substance, or commits any act against morals at the Workplace.

7. If the worker commits a verbal, physical, or other form of assault punishable by legislation in force in the UAE against the Employer, the responsible manager, his supervisor, or co-worker.

8. If the worker absents from Work without cause or justification acceptable to the Employer for more than (20) twenty interrupted days in a year, or more than (7) seven consecutive days.

9. If, the worker abuses his position with the aim to obtain personal gains, and profits.

10. If the worker joins another Establishment without complying with the controls and procedures prescribed in this regard.

WORKER MAY QUIT WITHOUT NOTICE

Article 45 describes the events where The worker may quit work without notice and reserve all his entitlements at the end-of-service.

Following are the events for which a worker may quit without notice:

a) If the Employer commits a breach of his obligations to the worker stated in the employment contract or this Decree Law or its implementing resolutions, the worker must notify the Ministry at **least (14) fourteen working days** before the date of leaving the Work. If the Employer is not able to remedy the breach despite being notified by the Ministry, then the worker may quit the job.

b) If the worker is subject to assault, violence, or harassment at the Workplace by the Employer or his legal representative, then the worker must report such acts to the concerned authorities and the Ministry **within (5) five Working Days** from the date on which he is able to report.

c) If the Workplace poses a serious threat to the safety or health of the worker, then the worker may quit the job. However, there are conditions which are as follows:

1. The employer must be aware of such serious threat, and

2. has not taken the actions necessary to eliminate such a threat.

Article 26 of the Executive Regulations determines the requirements for serious threats, which are as follows, allowing workers to leave work without warning

1. The presence of a potential source of ignition.

2. Exposure to electrical wires connected to a power source can cause electric shock or death.

3. The presence of dangerous chemicals that can cause diseases.

4. Unusual temperatures that cause burns.

5. Exposure to high noise that may harm the sense of hearing permanently.

6. Radiation that can cause cancer or blindness.

7. Biological hazards that can cause diseases.

8. If the Employer entrusts the worker with work that is substantially different from the work agreed-upon in the employment contract, without the written consent of the worker, except in cases stated in Article (12) hereof.

Termination of Contract During Probation

- The Employer may terminate the worker during the Probation period by giving the worker (14) fourteen day's prior written notice.

Employment contract may be terminated due to the bankruptcy or insolvency of the employer.

Article (25) of the executive regulation describes the events in which an employment contract may be terminated due to the bankruptcy or insolvency of the employer. As per this Article, subject to the provisions contained in Federal Decree Law No. (9) of 2016 regarding bankruptcy, Federal Decree Law No. (19) of 2019 regarding insolvency, and the provisions of Clause No. (8) of Article No. (42) of the Decree Law:

1. The employment contract shall be terminated in any of the following cases:

   a) Issuance of a court ruling for the bankruptcy or insolvency of the employer, in accordance with the legislation in force in the country in this regard.

   b) Issuance of a decision by the concerned authorities stating that the employer is unable to continue his activity for exceptional economic reasons, beyond his control.

2. The Ministry may, on its own, cancel the worker's work permit based on a judicial ruling declaring the employer's bankruptcy, and it may issue a new permit to him in accordance with the approved regulations in this regard.

TERMINATION OF EMPLOYMENT FOR MEDICAL UNFITNESS (Article 46)

The Employer may not terminate the Worker for medical unfitness before the Worker

1. Exhausts all his legal leaves and

2. Any agreement contrary to this shall be void, even if it preceded the entry into force of the provisions of this Decree Law.

ARBITRARY DISMISSAL (Article 47)

Article 47 prohibits an employer from terminating a worker if

1. if the Worker submits a serious complaint to the Ministry, or

2. files an action, proven to be valid, against the Employer.

An employer should not dismiss a worker solely because the worker submits complaints against the employer.

A dismissal of a worker by his employer in the situation of the above-mentioned condition shall be arbitrary.

The Employer shall pay the worker a fair compensation, estimated by a competent court, if it is found that dismissal is arbitrary.

The amount of compensation shall be determined based on the type of work, the extent of harm sustained by the worker, and the length of his service.

Cap on Maximum Compensation

In any case, the amount of compensation **shall not exceed three month's wage** of the worker, calculated based on the last wage received by him.

In addition to compensation, the worker shall be eligible to receive pay in lieu of notice and severance pay, due to him under the provisions hereof.

Chapter -XI
Individual Labour Disputes

Article 54 of the decree law and Article 31 of the Executive regulations deal with the individual labour dispute.

In the event of a dispute arising between the Employer and the Worker, or anyone claiming through them, in connection with any rights arising to either of them under the provisions hereof, they shall file an application to the Ministry, which shall consider the application and take whatever action necessary to settle the dispute between them amicably.

In the event that an amicable settlement is not possible, the Ministry shall refer the dispute to the competent court within (14) fourteen days from the date of submitting the request, and the referral shall be accompanied by a memorandum containing a summary of the dispute, the arguments of both parties, and the ministry's recommendation.

The competent court shall, within (3) three Working Days of the receipt of the application, set a hearing to consider the action and summon the litigants thereof, and shall promptly decide thereon.

The competent court shall dismiss the action if the procedures set out, above are not followed.

The worker shall have the right to claim two month's wages if he continues to work during the validity of the labour dispute referred to the judiciary. In this case, the Ministry may compel the employer to pay that wage, or refer the complaint in this regard to the judiciary.

Every worker whose complaint has been referred to the judiciary must register his case and quickly amend his status in the country.

The Minister may issue the necessary decisions regulating the status of the worker and the facility after referring the complaint to the judiciary.

An Individual Labour Dispute shall be treated as a dispute between the Establishment and the worker, and no penalties may be imposed, nor any administrative procedures may be taken against the Establishment in such a manner as to cause, harm to the other Workers of the Establishment or the employer unless after the settlement of the dispute or its resolution according to the provisions of this Decree Law and its Executive Regulations.

As an exception to this paragraph, the Ministry may, during the proceedings, oblige the Employer to continue to pay the worker's wage for a maximum period of two months, if the dispute results in the discontinuance of wages of the worker pursuant to the Executive Regulations.

Other administrative procedures or measures may be imposed on the Establishment by decision of the Minister, in order to prevent that the individual dispute results in a collective labour dispute and harm to the public interest.

An action for any rights arising under the provisions hereof shall not be heard after the expiry of one year from the due date of such claimed right.

This is modified by Federal Decree Law No. (9) of 2024, Federal Decree Law No. (33) of 2021

Employer and the Employee or their beneficiaries under the provisions of this Decree Law, the dispute shall be submitted to the Ministry for resolution. This application will be examined by the Ministry, and the necessary steps will be taken in order to resolve the dispute amicably.

The Ministry shall have jurisdiction to resolve the dispute by a decision in all cases involving disputes whose value does not exceed Dhs 50,000 (Fifty thousand dirhams) or whose dispute is concerning either party failing to adhere to an amicable settlement decision previously issued by the Ministry, regardless of the claim's value.

In accordance with paragraph No. 2 herein, the decision of the Ministry rendered to adjudicate the dispute shall be regarded as an executive bond and stamped with the executive formula in accordance with the usual procedure. Both parties to the dispute are entitled to file a lawsuit within (15) fifteen working days following notification or announcement of the decision before the competent court of first instance. The court shall schedule a hearing within three working days of the date the case is filed, notify the parties to the dispute of the hearing date, and decide the case within thirty (30) working days of the filing date. In accordance with this paragraph, the ruling of the competent court of first instance in the subject of the dispute shall be the final ruling. Upon filing the lawsuit, the Ministry's decision referred to in this provision will be suspended.

The Ministry shall refer the dispute to the appropriate court if no amicable settlement could be reached within the time frame prescribed in the Implementing Regulation of this Decree Law. The dispute shall be accompanied by a memorandum summarising the dispute, the party's arguments, and the Ministry's recommendations.

If the dispute continues, the Ministry may order the employer to pay the employee's wage for a maximum period of (2) two months, provided that the dispute has resulted

in the withholding of such payment in accordance with the provisions of this Decree Law's Implementing Regulation.

According to the Minister, other administrative measures or arrangements may be taken against the Establishment in order to prevent turning the current Individual Labour Dispute into a Collective Labour Dispute that might prejudice public interests.

Accordingly, the Court shall schedule a hearing within three (3) days to examine the lawsuit, notify the parties of the date of the hearing, and dispose of the matter in a summary manner.

No lawsuit pertaining to one of the disputes mentioned in this article shall be accepted without following the procedures and deadlines stipulated in this article.

Litigation concerning any of the rights accrued under this Decree Law may not be considered after two years from the date of termination of employment.

EXEMPTION FROM JUDICIAL FEES (55)

Labour actions shall be exempted from judicial fees at all stages of litigation and execution, and for applications filed by workers or their heirs up to AED 100,000 (UAE Dirhams One Hundred Thousand).

The Cabinet may, upon proposal of the Minister, increase or decrease the sum referred to in paragraph (1) above,.

COLLECTIVE LABOUR DISPUTES

Article 56 of the decree law and Article 32 of the Executive regulations deal with the collective labour dispute. The following are the main provisions:

In the event of a dispute arising between the Employer and all the workers, or group of them, and in case of failure of amicable settlement, the Employer or the workers may file a complaint with the Ministry pursuant to the controls and procedures specified by the Executive Regulations of this Decree Law.

The complainant, as mentioned above, must file a complaint in accordance with the following controls and procedures:

a) To submit the complaint through the channels specified by the Ministry.

b) To indicate the type and value of claims.

c) The complaint should be submitted within two weeks from the date of the dispute.

1. The Ministry may address the concerned authorities to impose a precautionary attachment on the facility to guarantee the rights of workers.

2. The ministers may liquidate the bank guarantee or insurance allocated to the workers without the need for the employer's approval if the worker's claim is proven to be true, or take any other measures to ensure the payment of worker's entitlements.

The Minister may impose administrative measures or procedures against the Establishment to prevent that any existing collective dispute, results in harm to the public interest.

The Ministry, in accordance with the procedures determined by a decision of the Minister, shall settle the dispute. In the event that settlement is not possible for any reason, or the parties are not committed to the agreed settlement, the dispute shall be referred to the Collective Labour Disputes Committee.

The Cabinet shall, upon proposal of the Minister, establish one or more committees called (Collective Labour Disputes Committee) to consider the collective labour disputes that cannot be resolved by the Ministry amicably. Such decision shall determine the formation, functions, mode of work and mechanism for issuance and implementation of decisions of the committee and other provisions regulating the smooth progress of work before the committee.

The collective labour dispute committees, formed by a decision of the Cabinet based on the proposal of the Minister, shall decide on the disputes referred to them. Their decision shall be final and appended by exequatur form by the competent court.

Chapter-XII

Labour Inspection (57)

Article 57 of the decree law and Article 33 of the Executive regulations deal with labour inspection. Following are the main provisions.

Employees of the Ministry entrusted by decision of the Minister of Justice, in agreement with the Minister, shall acquire the status of judicial officers in establishing any violation of the provisions of this Decree Law and its Executive Regulations and implementing resolutions, and shall have the right to access the relevant Establishment, detect violations and make reports in this regard.

As per the executive regulation of this decree,

1. Labour inspection shall be undertaken by specialised inspectors from among the Ministry's employees, and they shall have the following powers and functions:

   a) To monitor the proper implementation of the provisions of the Decree Law, this Resolution, and the legal regulations, especially those related to work conditions, wages, safety, and protection of workers while they perform their work.

   b) To provide employers and workers with information and technical guidance that will enable them to follow the best means to implement the provisions of the Decree Law and this Resolution.

2. Facts that are committed in violation of the provisions of the Decree Law, this Resolution, and the legal regulations, shall be seized according to the following procedures:

   a) If the inspector verifies during his inspection that there is a violation of the Decree Law, the regulations, or its executive decisions, he shall write a report to prove his awareness of the violation and submit it to the competent authority to take the necessary measures towards the violator.

   b) The labour inspector may, when necessary, request the competent administrative or security authorities to provide the necessary assistance.

   c) Violations are caught and registered by the inspectors in accordance with the mechanisms, regulations, channels, and forms decided by the Ministry.

   d) Employers and their representatives shall provide the inspectors assigned to inspect the work with the facilities and data necessary to perform their duty, to respond to requests, to appear before them, or to send a representative on their behalf if requested to do so.

3. The Minister may issue the necessary mechanisms to organise the work of the inspectors and the inspection procedures.

Articles 59 to 64 prescribe various penalties that can be imposed. However, as per Article 58, these penalties shall not prejudice any severe penalty provided for in another law.

Article (59)

Shall be sentenced to a fine of no less than AED 20,000 (UAE Twenty Thousand) and not more than AED 100,000 (UAE Dirhams One Hundred Thousand), whoever:

1. Provides false information or a document with the intent to bring a foreigner to the UAE for employment.

2. Obstructs or prevents any employee entrusted with the implementation of the provisions of this Decree Law and its Executive Regulations and implementing resolutions, or attempts or tries to prevent him from the discharge of his functions, whether by force, violence, or threat.

3. Divulges any business secret acquired by him in the course of his work as a public official entrusted with the implementation of the provisions of this Decree Law and its Executive Regulations and implementing resolutions, even if he leaves the work.

Article-60

Shall be sentenced to a fine of no less than AED 100,000 (UAE one hundred thousand) and not more than AED 1,000,000 (UAE Dirhams one million), whoever:

1. Employs a worker who has not obtained a permit to work for him.

2. Recruits or employs a worker and leaves him without Work.

3. Uses Work Permits for purposes, other than those for which they are issued.

4. Closes or ceases the activity of an Establishment without taking the procedures for settlement of worker's entitlements, in violation of the provisions of this Decree Law, its Executive Regulations, and implementing resolutions.

5. Employs a juvenile in violation of the provisions hereof.

6. Agrees to the employment of a Juvenile in violation of the provisions of this Decree Law in respect of the juvenile's parent or guardian.

Employers who commit violations of laws, regulations, or decisions governing the labour market and appoint an employee or employees in fictitious circumstances will be fined not less than 100,000 (one hundred thousand dirhams) and not more than 1,000,000 (one million dirhams) if such action results in the worker obtaining any benefit or advantage from any ministry, council, fund, authority, or any other government entity under which jurisdiction has been granted by law or decisions issued by the Council of Ministers for regulating the labour market, increasing the competitiveness of those employed in it, or assisting him in evading the fulfilment of statutory obligations. The employer may not recover the value of the financial incentives he paid to any of these entities from the employee, and the penalty stipulated in this clause is multiplied by the number of fictitious employees appointed.

1. In accordance with paragraph (2) of this Article, criminal proceedings may only be initiated at the Minister's or his authorised representative's request.

2. If the employer requests a settlement regarding the crime described in paragraph (2) herein, the Ministry may make a settlement prior to a judgement being rendered. The employer shall be required to pay at least 50% of the minimum fine specified for this offence as part of this agreement. Additionally, the employer must refund all financial incentives received by his employees who have been appointed fictitiously. The criminal case will be terminated upon the payment of the reconciliation amount.

3. In accordance with paragraph (3) of Article (54) of Federal Decree Law No. 33 of 2021 regarding labour relations, all disputes, grievances, and requests must be directed by the courts of appeal to the competent court of first instance in its current state without fees.

4. Disputes that have been adjudicated or are reserved for judgement are not subject to the provisions of paragraph No. (1) of this Article.

Article-61

Shall be sentenced to detention for a term of not less than (1) one year and/or a fine of not less than AED 200,000 (UAE Dirhams Two Hundred Thousand) and not more than AED 1,000,000 (UAE One Million), whoever abuses or misuses, or otherwise permits a third party to abuse or misuse, the online credentials allocated to him to login to the Ministry's systems, which results in disruption of labour relations or procedures.

Article-62

The fine imposed hereunder shall be multiplied for Employers by the number of workers in respect of whom the violation has occurred, subject to a maximum of AED 10,000,000.

Article-63

Shall be sentenced to a fine of not less than AED 5,000 (UAE Dirhams Five Thousand) and no more than AED 1,000,000 (UAE Dirhams One Million), whoever violates any other provisions of this Decree Law and its Executive Regulations, and implementing resolutions.

Article-64

In case of repetition of any of the violations referred to in this Decree Law and its Executive Regulations and implementing resolutions, before the lapse of (1) one year from being convicted for a similar violation, the offender shall be sentenced to detention and/or a fine equal to double the amount of the fine prescribed herein

Article (34)

Administrative Penalties

Subject to the provisions of Articles Nos. 58, 59, 60, 61, 62, 63, and 64 of the Decree Law, and in the event of a violation of the obligations stipulated in the Decree Law and this Resolution, the Ministry shall be granted the powers to impose administrative penalties as stated in Article 3 of the aforementioned Federal Law No. 14 of 2016 by Decree Law.

APPEAL AGAINST THE MINISTRY'S DECISIONS

Article 69 of the Decree law and Article 35 of the Executive Regulations of this Decree Law describe the process and procedures for appeal against the decision of the Ministry.

Both parties to a labour relation may appeal the decisions issued by the Ministry in accordance with the procedures, set by the Executive Regulations of this Decree Law

Procedures for grievances against the decisions of the Ministry

The two parties to the working relationship may submit a grievance against the decisions issued by the Ministry in accordance with the following procedures:

The request shall be submitted through the channels specified by the Ministry to its Grievance committee within (30) thirty days from the date of becoming aware of the decision.

The grievance request must include all data and documents supporting the grievance request.

Chapter-XIII

Mandates of the Cabinet (Article-70)

For the purposes of this Decree Law, the Cabinet shall have the following mandates:

1. Adopt conditions, controls and procedures for the classification of Establishments that are governed by the provisions of this Decree Law, and the privileges provided to each category of such Establishments.

2. Adopt conditions, controls, and procedures for the classification of the skill levels of manpower in the labour market governed by the provisions of this Decree Law and the privileges provided to each of such levels.

3. Adopt conditions, controls, and procedures for the employment of students of educational institutions accredited in the UAE in such a manner as to promote the labour market efficiency, and manpower competitiveness and enable employers to benefit from human capabilities.

4. Adopt conditions and controls for the employment of persons with special needs (People of Determination) in positions appropriate to their physical, intellectual, and technical capacities, determine their rights, obligations, and privileges, in a manner that contributes to their empowerment and engagement in the development path, and encourage Employers to employ them and provide them with all means of support and empowerment.

5. Adopt policies, legislation, and regulations that would regulate the labour market in the UAE, promote the contribution of Emiratis to the labour market, and urge Employers to recruit and employ Emiratis.

6. Issue decisions that would minimise the effects of any general exceptional circumstances facing the UAE in the labour sector in the UAE.

7. Change terms, rates or values stated in this Decree, depending on the labour market changes and needs, and as dictated by the public interest.

8. Determine the fees necessary for the implementation of the provisions of this Decree Law and its Executive Regulations.

MANDATES OF THE MINISTRY (Article 71)

For the purposes of this Decree Law, the Ministry shall have the following mandate:

1. propose policies, strategies and legislation in respect of:

   a) encouraging and urging establishments to invest in worker training and empowerment, and upgrading their skill levels, competency, and productivity.

   b) adopting modern techniques and technologies, and recruiting the best talents in accordance with the needs of the UAE's labour market, in order to improve productivity.

   c) training students of public and higher education institutions accredited in the UAE.

2. Put in place uniform templates for regulating the labour relations in establishments, and issue controls and mechanisms for their approval, in the interest of the worker and employer.

Chapter- XIV

Appendix

Recent amendment in Decree Law and Executive resolutions

1. UAE Ministerial Decision No. 46 of 2022 Regarding Work Permits, Job Offers, and Employment Contract's Forms: effective 3 February 2022

   A. Under this decision, employers must ensure that:

   - Parties execute an MOHRE standard form employment contract, which must conform with the offer letter provided. Additional provisions more beneficial to the employee, not otherwise stated in the offer letter, may be added. Addendums to the contract may also be agreed.

   - Maintain a digital or hard copy of both the offer letter and contract for a minimum period of two years from the date of termination.

   - Highlight to the employee their contractual rights and obligations.

   B. Employers will not be considered late in issuing or renewing a work permit in the following instances:

   - Where the employee has been out of the country for more than six months, and his/her residency visa expired while outside the country, and the work permit expired following the date of departure;

- Where the work permit expired following legal deportation or arrest.

- Where the employee dies, or contracts a contagious disease preventing the employee from working.

- Where an employee complaint has been referred by MOHRE to the Labour Court, and the work permit expires after the matter is referred.

- Where the employee leaves the UAE during the settlement period.

- Where the work permit expires during a period of imprisonment or detention; and,

- For a period of three months following the employer's death (being a sole manager), until a legal representative is appointed to manage the establishment.

C. Employers who fail to pay fines for non-compliance will not be permitted to renew or obtain new work permits until such fines are paid.

2. *UAE Ministerial Decision No. 44 of 2022: effective 3 February 2022*

This decision confirms the obligations under the Labour Law and its Implementing Regulations and provides that:

- An employer in the industrial sector or an employer with 100 employees or more must have an HSE officer to identify risks and mitigate against them;

- Working in exposed areas will be prohibited each year between 15 June and 15 September, from 12.30 pm to 3 pm;

- Employers with 50 employees or more earning AED 1500 or less must provide accommodation for such employees, which meets the requirements of Cabinet Decision 13 of 2019 and Ministerial Decision 212 of 2014; and

- The MOHRE will issue further decisions, setting out HSE obligations.

3. *UAE Ministerial Decision No. 47 of 2022 on Regulating Labour Disputes and Complaints Procedures: effective 4 February 2022.*

Under this decision, a complaint may be submitted by either the employer or employee within 30 days of the alleged breach. The MOHRE has 14 days to resolve the dispute; failing which, it should then be referred to the labour courts.

Where the complaint is made by the employee, the employee:

- Is required to record his complaint/claim with the Labour Court within 14 days of MOHRE's referral approval;

- May not work for another employer without obtaining a permit from MOHRE once the complaint is referred to the Labour Court; and,

- Is required to submit an application to MOHRE to cancel their original work permit within 14 days from the issuance of the final judgement of the dispute, where their employment relationship is terminated.

An employee may obtain a temporary work permit with their new employer while their claim with the Labour Court is pending, except in instances where a complaint for absconding is recorded.

Where the claim leads to the employee being suspended, the employee's work permit shall be cancelled on completion of six months post referral to the court.

Employees may request MHRE to cancel their work permit without the employer's consent. In such instances, MHRE will cancel the work permit in accordance with Article 5 of the decision.

Employers are required to report employee absence from work for a period of 7 consecutive days or more. In addition to administrative penalties that may be imposed, should the employer be found by MHRE to be in breach of complaints made, it may stop the issuance of new work permits for such period it deems appropriate.

This decision also contains a process for a collective dispute raised by 100 employees or more.

- May not work for another employer without obtaining a permit from MHRE once the complaint is referred to the Labour Court; and,

- Is required to submit an application to MHRE to cancel their original work permit within 14 days from the issuance of the final judgement of the dispute, where their employment relationship is terminated.

An employee may obtain a temporary work permit with their new employer while their claim with the Labour Court is pending, except in instances where a complaint for absconding is recorded.

Where the claim leads to the employee being suspended, the employee's work permit shall be cancelled on completion of six months post referral to the court.

4. UAE Ministerial Decision No. 48 of 2022 Regulating Labour Inspection Procedures: effective 4 February 2022

The decision sets out various controls and monitoring powers MHRE Labour Inspectors have, including entering the establishment, summoning employers, carrying out investigations, requiring data or information to be provided by the employer. It also sets out the inspector's obligations, including impartiality, avoiding any conflict of interest, and confidentiality with regard to the information provided and which comes to his knowledge as a result of his work.

5. *UAE Ministerial Decision No. 51 of 2022 on Licensing and Regulating the Activities of Recruitment Agencies: effective 7 February 2022*

This decision sets out the requirements and conditions for obtaining a recruitment agency licence, and the agency's obligations once the licence is obtained.

6. *UAE Ministerial Decision No. 43 of 2022 Regarding Wages Protection System: effective 15 February 2022*

All establishments registered with the MHRE must pay their employees through the WPS, with the following conditions:

- An employee's wage is due on the first day of the month following the registered payday in the employment contract;

- If wages are not paid within 15 days of the due date, the payment will be considered late (unless specified otherwise in the employment contract), and penalties imposed as set out in this decision (e.g., suspension of new permits on the 17th day of non-payment and non-renewal of existing permits from the 60th day of non-payment).

Companies are considered compliant with WPS:

- Where they pay a minimum of 90% of their workforce through WPS, and

- Employees receive a minimum of 80% of their wage, as set out in their employment contract, subject to proof of deduction being provided.

- Any agreement to a period of unpaid leave is communicated to MHRE.

The following employee categories are exempt from WPS:

- Employees who have filed a wage complaint with the Labour Court;

- Employees who have been reported to the Ministry as absent (absconder);

- New employees, up to 30 days from their wage due date; and

- Employees on unpaid leave, provided supporting documents are submitted to the MHRE.

The following employer categories are exempt from WPS:

- UAE national-owned fishing boats;

- UAE national-owned public taxis;

- Banks; and

- Houses of worship.

Employers had a grace period of three months to comply (from 15 February 2022).

7. ***Cabinet Decision no. (21) of 2020 on the fees of services and the administrative fines at the Ministry of Human Resources and Emiratisation, effective 5 April 2022.***

This decision sets out the fees payable for various applications to the MHRE and also the penalties for breaches of various obligations under the Labour Law, its Implementing Regulations, and the various decisions issued by the MHRE. Key penalties include the following:

Obligation Breached	Applicable Administrative Fine (AED),
Ghost or false Emiratisation,	20,000 per UAE national.
False information to WPS to circumvent the system.	5,000 per worker, up to a cap of 50,000
Failure to pay through WPS in line with requirements.	1,000 per worker, up to a cap of 20,000
Providing housing that is not compliant with requirements,	2,000 per worker
Obliging worker to pay recruitment fees.	5,000 per worker
Breaching procedures for employment or termination of UAE nationals.	20,000 per worker
Submitting incorrect documents or data to the MHRE to obtain any service or benefit.	2,000 per case

8. *Ministerial Decision No. 203/2022 on the regulation of granting electronic work permit quotas to establishments, effective 15 April 2022.*

This decision sets out quotas for employers obtaining electronic work permits. Quotas change depending on whether the employer is classified as being within an economic sector with high priority (as set out in the annexure to the decision) and also whether the employer is a new establishment or an existing establishment.

9. *Cabinet Decision No. 46 of 2022 on the establishment of a collective labour disputes committee: effective 9 May 2022*

This decision establishes a collective labour disputes committee, stipulates its members, and mandates it to hear disputes brought collectively by 50 employees or more. Once the committee is formed, it must schedule a hearing within two days of its receipt of the complaint. At the hearing, the workers may be represented by between 3-5 representatives from the complaining group, and the committee is obliged to provide its decision within 30 days of its hearing.

10. ***Ministerial Decision No. 208 of 2022 on the standards of determination of high-risk establishments, effective 1 June 2022***

Under this decision, the MHRE has created a 'high-risk' designation for employers who are in breach of their obligations. An employer will be at 'high-risk' if it falls into any of the following circumstances:

- Companies with 50 or more employees, who delay paying their employee wages under WPS.

- Termination of a number of employees, or a number of collective disputes being raised in the preceding 12-month period alleging breach of legal or contractual obligations.

- Employee complaints are being referred by MHRE to judicial entities, where 30% of the workforce has complained.

- 30% or more of the workforce have an expired work permit, and the employer does not renew within the required time limits.

- 30% or more of the workforce subject to interruption.

11. ***Cabinet Decision No. 18/2022 on the Classification of Private Sector Establishments Subject to the Provisions of the Law Regulating Labour Relation: effective 1 June 2022***

This decision repeals the previous law (Decision No. 26/2010) and resets the criteria companies must meet in order to be allocated into category one, two, and three of the classification system, as follows:

Category One

Employers must be 100% compliant with the UAE Labour Law, its executive regulations, and MHRE decisions and meet one of the following criteria:

- Raise its Emiratisation rates annually, in accordance with Cabinet resolutions, at a rate not less than 3 times the target;

- Cooperate with the new MHRE Emiratisation scheme, Nafis, in hiring and training at least 500 UAE nationals each year;

- Be classified as a small and medium-sized enterprise of young Emirati nationals;

- Be classed as a training and employment centre that supports the implementation of manpower policies, through the promotion of cultural and demographic diversity within the labour market;

- Fall within a targeted economic sector and activity as determined by the Cabinet; or,

- Fall within a Higher Corporation for Specialised Economic Zones (Zone Corp) establishment.

Category Two

Employers must:

- Comply with the UAE Labour Law, its executive regulations, and MHRE decisions; and,

- Comply with manpower policies through the promotion of cultural and demographic diversity within the labour market.

In addition:

- Establishments with 50 or more employees will fall into the second category and will need to comply with the requirement under 3b above, within a 'transitional period' yet to be determined by the Ministry of Finance.

- New establishments (regardless of size) shall initially fall into the second category and will remain subject to compliance with the criteria.

Category Three

Employers who

- Those who do not comply with manpower policies by promoting cultural and demographic diversity within the labour market; or,

- Those who have violated the UAE Labour Law, its executive regulations, and MHRE decisions, will fall into the third category.

12. ***Ministerial Decision No. 209/2022 on the classification of establishments under the third category: effective 1 June 2022***

    This decision sets out the minimum periods for which an employer will remain in category 3 under the employer classification system, with the period being linked to the employer's non-compliance. The periods run from at least 3 months, up to 2 years for the most serious of breaches.

www.ingramcontent.com/pod-product-compliance
Lightning Source LLC
Chambersburg PA
CBHW021225130726
47988CB00002B/827